David Copperfield

A play

Matthew Francis

Adapted from the novel by Charles Dickens

Samuel French — London
New York - Toronto - Hollywood

DAVID COPPERFIELD

First presented at the Greenwich Theatre, London, on 5th December 1997 with the following cast of characters:

David Copperfield	Damien Matthews
Young David	Paul Bailey

BLUNDERSTONE, SUFFOLK

Mama	Gemma Page
Peggotty	Miranda Kingsley
Mr Chillip	David Allister
Barkis	Brian Poyser
Mr Murdstone	Peter Hugo-Daly
Quinion	Joseph Millson
Passnidge	Des McAleer

YARMOUTH

Mr Peggotty	David Allister
Ham Peggotty, his nephew	Edward Waters
Little Emily, his niece	Eleanor Tremain

SALEM HOUSE

Mr Mell	David Allister
Mr Creakle	Des McAleer
Tungay	Peter Hugo-Daly
Thomas Traddles	Edward Waters
James Steerforth	Joseph Millson

LONDON

Mr Micawber	Des McAleer
Mrs Micawber	Miranda Kingsley
Creditor	Brian Poyser

DOVER

Aunt Betsey Trotwood	Susan Porrett
Mr Dick	Brian Poyser
Janet	Melanie Jessop

CANTERBURY
Mr Wickfield   David Allister
Agnes Wickfield   Eleanor Tremain
Uriah Heep   Peter Hugo-Daly
Dora Spenlow   Gemma Page

HIGHGATE
Mrs Steerforth   Susan Porrett
Rosa Dartle   Melanie Jessop

Servants, waiters, mariners, passers-by, coach passengers, schoolboys, thieves, second-hand clothes salesmen, warehouse workers played by members of the company.

Directed by Matthew Francis
Designed by Lez Brotherston
Music by Mia Soteriou
Lighting by Robert Bryan

CHARACTERS

David Copperfield
Young David
Mama
Peggotty
Mr Chillip
Barkis
Mr Murdstone
Quinion
Passnidge
Mr Peggotty
Ham Peggotty, his nephew
Little Emily, his niece
Mr Mell
Mr Creakle
Tungay
Thomas Traddles
James Steerforth
Mr Micawber
Mrs Micawber
Bailiff
Aunt Betsey Trotwood
Mr Dick
Janet
Mr Wickfield
Agnes Wickfield
Uriah Heep
Dora Spenlow
Mrs Steerforth
Rosa Dartle
Servants, Waiters, Mariners, etc.

The action takes place in various interior and exterior settings

Time—1820s-1840s

PRODUCTION NOTES

TELLING THE STORY

David Copperfield is an epic. Even in this adaptation — which has sacrificed a number of sub-plots and characters to keep the play at a single evening — the action covers many locations, three decades and innumerable twists and turns. The director and his actors will achieve their own rhythms for the piece, but I cannot put too great an emphasis on the need to shift from scene to scene with expedition and a minimum of interruption. At Greenwich, Lez Brotherston designed a brilliant many-levelled set, so that the play could drive ahead without the need for time-consuming scene changes. Characters for each scene would materialize in the shadows as the previous scene reached its conclusion; lights would shift audience attention from one part of the set to another; fresh items of furniture were incorporated as part of a new scene. Ingenious transitions were at a premium.

Of course, the pace of each scene would vary greatly, but there were never hold-ups *between* the scenes. This could be achieved in many other ways (a bare-boards production with the cast in view throughout for example), but the narrative drive must never be lost for the sake of cumbersome changes.

THE TWO DAVIDS

To dramatize the internal conflicts of the central character, I used the device of having *two* Davids on stage through much of the production. The younger David clings to the intense experiences of childhood, the older struggles to come to terms with different realities. This idea yielded far more dramatic and emotional power than I had expected, and the director and his/her actors should experiment with this relationship to see what subtleties can be achieved. I have indicated in the text some of the places where Young David is on stage watching, shadowing or interrupting the action of the second half — but if the director finds other places where Young David's presence can make a point, then s/he should feel free to develop these. The same applies to the older David's presence in Act I.

The difference in age between the two Davids is not great. The younger David *could* be played by a very gifted child, but we were lucky to have Paul Bailey — an eighteen-year-old actor who skilfully presented David between the ages of 0 and 12. The older David should be in his late 20s, early 30s.

The audience grasp this device very quickly after the I AM BORN scene, and similarities between the two actors can be enhanced by a clever designer and costume supervisor.

DOUBLING

At Greenwich and Sheffield, we presented the play with a cast of 13. Doubling is made clear in the original cast list on page iii. It would be possible to present the play with a bigger company of actors (there were 28 parts credited in our programme), but it would be hard to present it with a smaller cast. There are a number of ensemble scenes, which could be played by a much greater number of narrators and standers-by than I have indicated.

CUTS

Our production played at 3 hours with an interval. Audiences seemed well prepared for the Dickens's "feast", and it would be wrong to interfere too much with the "spread" of the novel. The script with which we started rehearsals was very much longer than the version we finally performed.

ACCENTS

It is worth putting in time on the Suffolk accent — a very particular and attractive sound — and not settling for a generalized Mummerset brogue. Tapes and CDs are readily available, and there are dialect coaches who can be contacted via the principal drama schools.

MUSIC

Incidental music for the production was composed by Mia Soteriou. It occurs where indicated in the script, and copies can be obtained on DAT or cassette tape on application to Rachel Daniels at London Management, 2-4 Noel Street, London W1V 3RB, UK (tel: +44 171 287 9000). Please note a performance/hire fee may be payable.

Three of the songs were original, with words by the adapter, and music by Mia Soteriou: these are "A Pretty Young Girl" in Act I, Scene 3; "The Cathedral School Song" in Act I, Scene 28; and the "Storm Choruses" in Act II, Scene 24. Sheet music is obtainable from Rachel Daniels at the address given above. Recordings of the "The School Song", and of the "Storm Choruses" are also available.

There is one traditional song used in the adaptation: "The Curragh of Kildare" in Act II, Scene 12. There are three Victorian ballads: "Ye Mariners of England" (Thomas Campbell) in Act II, Scene 4; "Annabel Lee" (Edgar Allen Poe) in Act II, Scene 7; and "List to the Convent Bells" (John Blockley) in Act II, Scene 23. All four of these songs are readily available in sheet music form from libraries and good music shops. Director's will find several of the songs in *Victorian Songs and Duets,* edited by Benjamin Luxon and Robert Tear, published by Cramer Music Ltd.

Matthew Francis

This adaptation is dedicated to
the future life of the Greenwich Theatre
and the loyal and dedicated team
who have made it such a success in the past.

" ... it so falls out
That what we have we prize not to the worth
Whiles we enjoy it, but being lacked and lost,
Why, then we rack the value, then we find
The virtue that possession would not show us
Whiles it was ours."
Much Ado About Nothing Act IV, Scene 1

Other plays by Matthew Francis
published by Samuel French Ltd:

The Adventures of Huckleberry Finn
(*from the novel by Mark Twain*)

Northanger Abbey
(*from the novel by Jane Austen*)

The Prisoner of Zenda
(*from the novel by Anthony Hope*)

A Tale of Two Cities
(*from the novel by Charles Dickens*)

ACT I

SCENE 1

THE LONG AND GLOOMY NIGHT

A small boy with a dim lamp in the middle of a lonely space

Young David (*calling out*) Mama! Mama! —Peggotty! Where are you hid?

We see the boy's older self at a desk going through papers. He is distracted, edgy. In the distance, the sound of a thunderstorm, which gets louder and louder

David The old unhappy loss or want of something always had some place in my heart ... I felt the void which somewhere seemed to be about me ... there was always something wanting ... always, always.

The noise of the storm is louder now. Voices call from the gloom. We can just make out the other members of the Company around him

Company (*variously*) David? /David, sir?/ Master Copperfield!/ No, no, I shall call you Daisy.../ I shall call you Trotwood Copperfield!/ It's Brooks of Sheffield!/ Doady, Doady my dearest.../ Davey, Mas'r Davey!/ Master Murdstone.../ Prig!.../ A common vagabond...

David has to fight the noise of the storm

David (*getting to his feet*) ... a murky confusion ... I was seriously affected — confused — there was that jumble in my thoughts and recollections that I had lost the sense of time, distance ... a great darkness besides ... terrors real and fanciful ... I could see nothing — only my own haggard face looking in at me from the *black void* ...

A sudden change. Brightness. Sunshine. Bird song. The prospect of sandy beaches and trees

Scene 2

I am Born

Blunderstone

Young David (*relieved, happy*) I am born!

Cheers, applause. The Company breaks up and goes its way. Young David runs behind his mother's skirts. She is very pregnant. Mr Chillip (the doctor) hovers. Betsey Trotwood confronts Mama

Aunt Betsey Mrs David Copperfield, I *think* ...
Mama (*faintly*) Yes.
Aunt Betsey (*slight bow*) Miss Trotwood. You have heard of her I dare say?
Mama (*not much of a pleasure*) I've had the pleasure. Oh dear ...
Aunt Betsey Now you see her.
Mama Oh dear. I mean ... oh no. Oh goodness.

Tears

Aunt Betsey Oh tut tut tut tut! Don't do that! Come, come!
David (*to the audience*) Betsey Trotwood was the principal magnate of our
      family, and had been married to a husband younger than herself. He had
      tried to throw her out of a window, and then left for India with his capital,
      where — according to a wild legend in our family — he was once seen
      riding on an elephant in company with a baboon.
Aunt Betsey (*impatiently*) Begum!
Young David Aunt Betsey Trotwood.
Aunt Betsey (*to Mama*) Take off your cap, child, and let me see you.

Mama does as told; a tumble of lovely hair

      (*Touching her hair with no ungentle hand*) Why, bless my heart! You are
      a very baby.
Mama Yes indeed. It is very hard. I am a childish widow. Yes. And shall be
      a childish mother if I live ...
David I was a posthumous child. How strange that my father never saw me.
Young David He is under the white gravestone. Is he lonely there?
Aunt Betsey (*brisk*) Stuff!
Mama Mr Copperfield is dead, and if you dare to speak unkindly of him—
Aunt Betsey (*ignoring her*) And when do you expect ...?

Mama I am all in a tremble. I shall die I am sure.
Aunt Betsey No no no. Have some tea.
Mama Will it do me any good?
Aunt Betsey Of course!
Mama Peggotty!

Peggotty is instantly there

Aunt Betsey (*to Peggotty*) It is hard to credit that any human being has gone
    into a Christian Church, and got herself named Peggotty.
Peggotty I ——
Aunt Betsey Tea. Don't dawdle.

Peggotty flees

Aunt Betsey Now child, from the moment of the birth of this girl ——
Mama Perhaps boy.
Aunt Betsey I have a presentiment that it must be a girl. Don't contradict.
    From the moment of this girl's birth, I intend to be her friend. I beg you'll
    call her Betsey Trotwood Copperfield. There must be no mistakes in life
    with *this* Betsey Trotwood. There must be no trifling with her affections ——

At this moment, Mama gives a loud scream and goes into a noisy labour

Chillip and Peggotty gather around her

*Chatter and fuss and flap. Aunt Betsey puts on a pair of ear muffs and screws
up her face at the noise. From under Mama's skirts, Chillip pulls Young
David, in an enormous blanket and cap*

Aunt Betsey (*removing ear muffs*) And how is she?
Chillip Quite as comfortable as we can expect a young mother to be under
    these melancholy domestic circumstances.
Aunt Betsey And *she.* How is *she*?
Chillip I'm afraid I don't ——
Aunt Betsey *The baby!* How is *she*?
Chillip Ma'am, I apprehended you had known. It's a boy.

A terrible moment

*Aunt Betsey takes her bonnet like a sling and aims a blow at Mr Chillip's
head. She gathers up her bags, and walks out*

They watch her departure

Young David Like a fairy.
David A discontented fairy.

Scene 3

Childhood and Crocodiles

Pipe music. Pretty, childhood music

Mama and Peggotty settle to housework. Mama is not very good at it

Mama Where are you, Davy?
David The old times. Precious, precious … what are they — the first things
   I remember?
Young David Hens. Big hens …
David Walking about in a menacing and ferocious manner …
Young David Geese. They come after me. I dream about them …
David As a man environed by wild beasts might dream of lions …
Young David *And crocodiles* …
Peggotty I ain't heard of them.
Young David They grow very big, sometimes ten foot long, and they float
   in the mud by the edge of the river, and they disappear under the water other
   times and you mustn't tread on them.
Peggotty And do you peel them?
Young David What?
Peggotty These Crorkindills — and is they best boiled or baked?
Young David Peggotty ——
Peggotty Like a marrow I suppose ——
Young David Peggotty!

Mama starts to sing

Mama   A pretty young girl to the orchard did go
                         And seventeen apples she picked from the tree,
                         She was sweet seventeen and had seventeen beaux
                         Oh which of you want to come walking with me …

Young David (*going to her*) Pretty.
David Nobody knows better than I do that she likes to look so well and is
   proud of being so pretty …

During the following verse, Mama dances with Young David

Barkis comes on to watch. He devotes a lot of attention to Peggotty as well

Mama (*singing*) Tom asked for an apple, and Jim asked for three,
             John gave her a sixpence for four,
             But the pick of the orchard was handsome Davy
             Oh he's the young man to go walking with me,
             He gave me a glittering golden guinea
             Yes, he's the young man I adore.

Barkis (*nodding at Peggotty*) Barkis is willin'...

Barkis goes

Young David watches him go

Young David Peggotty — were you ever married?
Peggotty Lord, Master Davy — What's put marriage in your head!
Young David But *were* you ever married, Peggotty? You are a very handsome woman, an't you?
David (*to the audience*) In a different style to my mother certainly, but of another school of beauty — I considered her a perfect example.
Peggotty *Me* handsome, Davy! Lawk no, my dear! But what put marriage in your head?
Young David I don't know. You mustn't marry more than one person at a time, may you, Peggotty?
Peggotty Certainly not.
Young David But if you marry a person and that person dies, why then you may marry another person, mayn't you Peggotty?
Peggotty You *may*, if you chose. That's a matter of opinion.
Young David But what is your opinion, Peggotty?
Peggotty (*this is awkward*) My opinion is ... that I never was married myself, Master Davy, and that I don't expect to be. That's all I know about the subject ... Now these Cronkindales ...

SCENE 4

MR MURDSTONE

Mama is talking with a group of three men: Murdstone, Quinion (a dark man with a dark voice), and Passnidge. She comes forward with Murdstone

Mama Davey!
Young David They are monsters — and they lay eggs in the sand ——

Mama Davy …

Young David And you can get away from them if you keep turning and turning, because they can't you see because they're stiff and awkward——

Mama This is a friend of mine …

Young David And you can sharpen sticks and put them down their throats —

Mama Mr Murdstone.

Murdstone Hallo Davy.

Young David And that kills them.

Mama (*hugging him*) Davy!

Murdstone He's a highly privileged little fellow.

Young David What does that mean?

Murdstone (*stooping to stroke Young David's hair, putting his arm round Mama*) To enjoy such favour.

Young David (*pushing him away from Mama*) Not today thank you.

Mama Oh *Davy*.

Murdstone I cannot wonder at his devotion.

Mama (*laughing*) Don't be so rude.

Murdstone You inspire it.

Mama Thank you for taking so much trouble to see me home. It's out of your way.

Murdstone Come, my fine boy, let us be the best friends in the world! Shake hands!

Young David (*giving him the wrong hand*) Good-night.

Mama (*laughing*) Why that's the wrong hand, Davy!

Young David (*persisting*) Good-night.

Mama Davy, give the gentleman your *right* hand

Murdstone (*shaking Davy's left hand*) No matter. He's a brave fellow. (*To Mama, kissing her hand*) Good-night.

She turns and moves with Peggotty to another part of the stage. Murdstone turns to his friends. David watches them

Quinion Bewitching.

Passnidge A pretty little widow.

Murdstone Take care if you please. Somebody's sharp.

Quinion Who is?

Murdstone (*staring at David*) Only Brooks of Sheffield.

Passnidge And what is the opinion of Brooks of Sheffield in reference to the projected business?

Murdstone I don't know that Brooks understands much about it at present, but he is not generally favourable I believe.

Laughter

They turn and go

There is the sound of horses trotting away. Young David turns back and finds his Mama and Peggotty in dispute

Mama Good heavens! You'll drive me mad. Was ever any poor girl so ill-used by her servants as I am! How can you have the heart to make me so uncomfortable and say such bitter things to me, when you are well aware that I haven't, out of this place, a single friend to turn to!

Young David Mama!

Peggotty The more's the reason for saying that it won't do. No! That it won't do. *No!* No price could make it do. *No!*

Mama I tell you — beyond the commonest civilities, nothing whatever has passed! You talk of admiration. What am I to do? Would you wish me to shave my head or disfigure myself with a burn or a scald or something of that sort? I dare say you would, Peggotty. I dare say you'd quite enjoy it!

Peggotty No no no!

Young David Stop it, stop it!

Mama And is it to be hinted that I am wanting in affection for my little Davy, my precious treasure, the dearest little fellow that ever was?

Peggotty Nobody never went and hinted no such thing!

Mama You did, Peggotty, you did! (*To Young David*) Am I a naughty Mama to you, Davy? Am I a nasty, cruel, selfish bad Mama?

Young David No!

Mama Say I am — say yes, dear child, and Peggotty will love you, and Peggotty's love is a great deal better than mine, Davy. *I* don't love you at all, do I?

Everyone in tears now; talking over each other

Young David Yes, yes you do, you do!

Peggotty And he knows it, ma'am.

Mama Was ever a poor girl treated in such a way …

Young David Peggotty, Peggotty, how could you! You're a beast, a *beast*!

Mama Don't say that, Davy. Don't call Peggotty a beast ——

Peggotty I am indeed, I'm a beast to make my dear mistress cry. A beast!

Young David No! You're my Peggotty.

Mama What's to become of me. What's to become of us …

And they collapse in a sobbing heap

SCENE 5

YARMOUTH

A fiddle strikes up, and a sailor song maybe. The sound of seagulls and a gentle noise of wind

David Two months later, Peggotty proposed a trip to Yarmouth to visit her brother ——

Mr Peggotty, Ham, and Emily arrive

Mr Peggotty Mr Peggotty.
David And her nephew ——
Ham Ham.
Emily And her niece — Little Em'ly.
David Just the two of us. Without being nearly so much surprised as I had expected, my mother entered into the plan readily.
Young David *Yarmouth!*
Peggotty What do you think of it?
Young David Flat.
Ham 'Tis that!

During the following, the boathouse is trundled/lowered into view. It is neat, clean and ingeniously laid out. Ham, Mr Peggotty and Emily sit down inside it

Young David And there an't no line where the sea begins.
Peggotty *(firmly)* We must take things as we find them. For my part — I'm proud to call myself a Yarmouth Bloater!
Ham Yon's our house, Mas'r Davy!
Young David *(after a beat)* That's not it? That ship-looking thing?
Ham That's it, Mas'r Davy.
Young David But it's a boat.
Ham And 'as sailed the seas for fifty years. But now it's coasted in to be a place for us to live!
Young David *(awed)* A real boat…
David If it had been Aladdin's palace, roc's egg and all, I suppose I could not have been more charmed with the romantic idea of living in it.
Mr Peggotty Glad to see you, sir. You'll find us rough, but you'll find us ready.
Young David Thank you. I know I shall be happy here. A real boat …
Mr Peggotty Will you have a bite of supper with us?

Ham Boiled dabs!
Emily (*shy*) 'Tatoes.
Peggotty And a chop for you, my darling.
Young David Cooking — in a *boat* ...
Mr Peggotty And eating too!

Plates and chatter. Spoons scrape plates clean

Young David Mr Peggotty!
Mr Peggotty Sir.
Young David Did you give your son the name of Ham, because you lived in a sort of ark?
Mr Peggotty No, sir. I never give him no name.
Young David Who gave him that name, then?
Mr Peggotty Why, sir, his father give it him.
Young David I thought you were his father!
Mr Peggotty My brother Joe was *his* father ...
Young David Dead, Mr Peggotty?
Mr Peggotty Drowndead.
Young David Little Em'ly. She is your daughter, isn't she, Mr Peggotty?
Mr Peggotty No, sir. My brother-in-law Tom was her father.
Young David (*a beat*) Dead, Mr Peggotty?
Mr Peggotty Drowndead.
Young David (*after several beats*) Haven't you *any* children, Mr Peggotty?
Mr Peggotty No, master, I'm a bacheldore.
Young David A bachelor! And you look after Ham and little Em'ly?
Peggotty He's as generous as any man in England.
Mr Peggotty (*warningly*) Clara ...
Peggotty Though he's but a poor man himself ——
Mr Peggotty (*crusty*) Clara! I'll be gormed if I don't cut and run for good — if ever you say such a thing again!

The Lights shift. A bright morning on the beach

Peggotty, Ham and Mr Peggotty leave

David The next day, Em'ly and I were strolling on the beach ...
Young David You're quite a sailor I suppose?
Emily No. I'm afraid of the sea.
Young David Afraid! I an't.
Emily It's cruel. I've seen it tear a boat as big as our house, all to pieces.
Young David I hope it wasn't the boat ——
Emily That Father was drowned in. No. I never see that boat.

Young David Nor him?

Emily Not to remember.

Young David My father died before I was born. My mother and Peggotty and I live by ourselves ...

Emily But my mother's dead too. She died before my father. Besides, your father was a gentleman and your mother is a lady; and my father was a fisherman and my mother was a fisherman's daughter.

Young David And would you like to be a lady?

Emily (*at once*) Oh yes. (*Beat*) I should like it very much. We would all be gentlefolks together then. We wouldn't mind then when there come stormy weather.

Young David Yes ...

Emily (*carefully*) Don't you think you're afraid of the sea, now?

Young David No. You don't seem to be either, though you say you are.

Emily I'm not afraid in the day. But I wake when it blows and tremble to think of Uncle Dan and Ham, and believe I can hear 'em crying out for help. That's why I should like so much to be a lady. But I'm not afraid in this way. Not a bit. Look here!

This is a big moment. Emily runs out into the audience, perhaps — along an old jetty, then on past the end of it, hopping from stone to stone. We hear the wind blow and a few notes of music. The lighting on Emily intensifies

David The incident is so impressed on my remembrance, that I could draw its form here — accurately as it was that day, and the light, bold, fluttering figure springing forward to her destruction!

Young David *No!*

Emily laughs, and runs back to him. The music fades. The lighting is restored. A beat. Idyll

Emily goes

SCENE 6

A NEW FATHER

David Of course I was in love with Little Em'ly. My agony of mind at leaving her was piercing.

A beat. The light grows chilly

Young David (*suddenly anxious*) Mama! Mama!!

Murdstone walks forward. Mama is behind him. Peggotty is with Young David

Murdstone Davy boy, how do you do.
Young David Ma!
Murdstone You have a new father.
Young David *No!*
Peggotty I should have told you before now.
Young David NO!
Peggotty But I couldn't bring my mind to it.
Mama (*going to him and hugging him*) Davy, Davy, my child!
Murdstone Now Clara, my dear; recollect! Control yourself, always control
  yourself.
Mama (*nervously*) Of course. Davy — whatever is the matter?

Davy cries and cries

Mama This is your doing, Peggotty, you cruel thing! How can you reconcile
  it to your conscience, I wonder, to prejudice my own boy against me, or
  against anybody who is dear to me?
Peggotty Lord forgive you, Mrs Copperfield ...
Mama It's enough to distract me, in my honeymoon, too ... Davy, you
  naughty boy! Peggotty, you savage creature.
Murdstone Clara, my love, have you forgotten? Firmness, my dear!
Mama (*mumbling*) I am very sorry, Edward.
Murdstone (*to Peggotty*) My friend — do you know your mistress's name?
Peggotty She has been my mistress a long time. I ought to know it.
Murdstone She has taken mine you know. Will you remember that?

Peggotty curtsies

  David, if I have an obstinate horse or dog to deal with, what do you think
  I do?
Young David I don't know.
Murdstone I beat him. I make him wince and smart. I say to myself, "I'll
  conquer that fellow"; and if it were to cost him all the blood he had, I should
  do it. Now — what are those marks on your cheek?
Peggotty Tears ——
Young David (*quickly*) Dirt.
Murdstone You have a good deal of intelligence for a little fellow, and you
  understand me very well, I see. Wash that face, sir, and come down
  presently.

*Young David runs off and away down to his room and flings himself on his
bed. David cannot reach him, cannot help him. He stretches out his arms. The
Lights come up on the two Davids*

David God help me! I might have been improved for my whole life, I might
have been made another creature perhaps, for life, by a kind word at that
season. A word of encouragement and explanation, of pity for my childish
ignorance, of welcome home, of reassurance to me that it *was* home,
might have made me dutiful to him, might have made me respect him
instead of ——
Young David — hate him.

SCENE 7

FAMILY LIFE

The Lights come up on a sitting-room area: the best parlour

Mama and Murdstone are there

David The days turned to weeks and the weeks to months. My mother
became more serious and thoughtful. Her face looked careworn and too
delicate, and her manner was anxious and fluttered.
Mama Oh pray, pray Edward, don't accuse me of being ungrateful. I have
many faults but not that! Oh don't, my dear!

Young David hears the quarrel and comes down to the door

Murdstone When my efforts are met with so base a return, that feeling of
mine is chilled and altered.
Mama (*faintly*) Pray let us be friends. I couldn't live under coldness or
unkindness. I am so sorry. I have a great many faults I know ——
Murdstone (*seeing the boy*) David! Where have you been? I will not have
the room shunned as if it were infected at the pleasure of a child. Sit down.

Young David does

SCENE 8

LESSONS

Young David opens books and papers. Murdstone has a cane

David These lessons — continued I suppose for six months or more — were the death-blow at my peace; long, numerous, hard, perfectly unintelligible. One morning, when I went into the parlour with my books, I found my mother looking anxious, and Mr Murdstone binding something round the bottom of a cane.

Murdstone If I go into a cheesemonger's shop, and buy 5000 double Gloucester cheeses at fourpence-halfpenny each, how much change will I have out of £100?

David, remembering, grabs a piece of paper and tries again to work out Murdstone's exercises

Young David Six pounds and, er — and er ——

Murdstone If my new dressing-gown costs twelve shillings and five pence, and I am to pay for the garment in farthings — how many will I need to give Mr Flimsy the tailor?

Young David Er — er... four hundred and er — er ——

Murdstone Through which countries does the river Danube flow?

Young David Seventy-four?

Murdstone Counties — Coastal — of England — name — now?

Young David Germany ...

Murdstone Plural past imperfect future indicative active gerund?

Young David Amantiboribis — bissimus — missibus ——

Murdstone Locusts — five million — poppy fields — eat — how many — rate of — in a day — book of the Bible — plagues divided into — son of Abraham — name — at once.

Young David Abel ...

Murdstone Hardly.

Young David Cain ...

Mama Oh Davy, Davy!

Murdstone Cane.

David Cane ...

Mama (*sobbing*) Edward — no

Murdstone I tell you, Clara — I have often been flogged myself.

Mama But — but do you think it did you good?

Murdstone Do you think it did me harm? (*Quick pause*) David, you and I will go upstairs, boy.

And he walks Young David out of the parlour and up to David's bedroom, then suddenly twists Young David's head under his arm

Young David Mr Murdstone! Sir! Don't. Pray don't beat me! I have tried to learn sir, but I can't learn when you are by. I can't indeed!

Murdstone Can't you indeed, David? We'll try that.

Murdstone lifts the cane, but Young David twists around and takes a bite at Murdstone's hand. It's a good bite. Murdstone yells, and then beats and beats Young David. Peggotty and Mama are hammering at the door and crying out. At last the beating stops and the door is slammed shut on Young David. The loud sound of the door being locked. The Lights focus on Young David: a sobbing heap on the floor

SCENE 9

IN PRISON

David My imprisonment lasted for five days. Oh, the length of those five days ...

We hear the soundtrack of the house as Young David notes each noise

Young David Bells ringing ... doors opening, shutting ... voices in the best parlour ... footsteps on the stairs ...

A sudden note of hope here, but the footsteps go past

   ... in the lane outside laughing singing ...

Young David joins in with a few notes of the song

   What time is it? ... Nearly dawn? ... Six, seven, eight, nine, ten ... Not midnight yet ... Rain.
David All this! All this! It appears to have gone round and round for years instead of days, it is so vividly and strongly stamped on my remembrance!

Peggotty is at the keyhole

Peggotty (*in a fearful whisper*) Davy! Davy!!
Young David Is that you, Peggotty?
Peggotty My own precious Davy! Be as soft as a mouse or the cat'll hear us!
Young David How's Mama, dear Peggotty? Is she very angry with me?
Peggotty (*crying*) No, no.
Young David Will I go to prison, will I be hanged?
Peggotty Lord bless us *no*!
Young David What is going to be done with me?

Peggotty School, near London. Place called Salem House …
Young David When, Peggotty?
Peggotty Tomorrow. (*Beat*) Davy dear — can you hear me?

Music underscore

Young David (*crying*) Yes, yes Peggotty.
Peggotty My own! (*In broken little sentences*) What I want to say is. That you must never forget me. For I'll never forget you. And I'll take as much care of your Mama, Davy. As ever I took care of you. And I won't leave her. The day may come when she'll be glad to lay her poor head. On her stupid, cross old Peggotty's arm again. And I'll write to you, my dear. Though I ain't no scholar. And I'll — I'll …
Young David Thank you, thank you, thank you. And Peggotty — will you write and tell Mr Peggotty and Little Em'ly that I am not as bad as they might suppose, and that I sent 'em all my love.

Music swells

David In the morning I ran into my mother's arms. But they had persuaded her that I was a wicked fellow.
Mama Oh Davy! That you could hurt anyone I love! Try to be better. Pray to be better! I forgive you; but I am so grieved, Davy, that you should have such bad passions in your heart.
Murdstone Clara!
Mama You are going for your own good. You will come home in the holidays and be a better boy. (*Sobbing*) Goodbye, my child!
Murdstone Clara!
Mama I forgive you, my dear boy. God bless you!
Murdstone CLARA!
David And so I lost her. So I lost her.

SCENE 10

BARKIS

The trotting of hooves. They belong to the horse of Barkis, the carrier. Young David and Barkis are jogging along. There are boxes and bags, including a school trunk

Young David Are you going all the way?
Barkis All the way where?

Young David There.

Barkis Where's there?

Young David Near London?

Barkis Why that horse would be deader than pork afore he got over half the ground.

Young David Are you only going to Yarmouth then?

Barkis That's about it. I shall take you to the stage-cutch, and the stage-cutch'll take you to — wherever it is.

Young David Will you have a cake, Mr Barkis?

Barkis does and swallows it in one "like an elephant"

Barkis Did *she* make 'em now?

Young David Peggotty do you mean, sir?

Barkis Ah, her.

Young David Yes, she makes all our pastry and does all our cooking.

Barkis Do she though? (*Beat*) No sweethearts I believe?

Young David Oh no. She never had a sweetheart.

Barkis Didn't she though? (*Beat*) So she makes all the apple parsties, and does all the cooking, do she?

Young David Yes indeed.

Barkis P'raps you might be writing to her.

Young David I shall certainly be writing to her.

Barkis Well, if you was writin' to her, p'raps you'd recollect to say that Barkis is willin', would you?

Young David That Barkis is willing. Is that all the message?

Barkis Ye-es. Ye-es. Barkis is willin, Barkis — is willin'.

Barkis retreats

Young David is left on his school trunk

Mr Mell appears

SCENE 11

SALEM HOUSE

David I was collected from the coach station by ——

Mr Mell Mr Mell. Hallo.

Young David Hallo.

Mr Mell Junior master — Salem House.

Young David If you please, sir — is it far?
Mr Mell Down by Blackheath.

Boys gather round. A huge blackboard is lowered in. Creakle, a villainous man with a cane, prowls in, followed by another, Tungay — a pegleg with a bull neck and surly face

David School began in earnest the next day.

Creakle raps his cane on to his desk. Two of the boys bring out a placard which reads "TAKE CARE OF HIM HE BITES". Young David looks around nervously

David The headmaster at Salem House was Mr Creakle. He had no voice, but spoke in a dreadful whisper.
Creakle (*in a hoarse whisper*) And what — Copperfield — are you looking for?
David A man with a wooden leg acted as his interpreter.
Tungay (*deafening*) What you lookin' for?
Young David If you please, sir, I'm looking for the dog.
Creakle Dog, says he. What dog?
Tungay What dog!
Young David Isn't it a dog, sir?
Creakle Isn't what a dog?
Tungay What a dog?
Young David That's to be taken care of, sir; that bites.
Creakle No, Copperfield, that's not a dog.
Tungay Not a dog.
Creakle That's a boy.
Tungay It's a boy ...
Creakle I have the happiness of knowing your father — Mr Murdstone. And a worthy man he is, and a man of strong character. His instructions are — to put this placard on your back.
Tungay Put the placard on his back!

Two of the boys strap the placard to David's back

Creakle Now, Master Copperfield — are you famous for biting?
Tungay Famous for biting?!
Creakle Well I'm famous for biting too. Do you see this cane?
Tungay The cane, yeees!
Creakle What do you think of that for a tooth — (*he swipes at David*) — is it a sharp tooth — (*he swipes again*) — is it a double tooth — (*he swipes*

again) — has it a deep prong — (*and again*) — does it BITE…! (*Swipe*)
Now boys! This is a new half at Salem House. Take care what you're about
in this new half. Come fresh up to lessons I advise you, for I come fresh up
to the punishment. I won't flinch! (*Back to David*) I'll tell you what I am.
I'm a tartar.

Tungay A tartar.

Creakle Right! *Amo, amas, amat!*

Boys *Amo, amas, amat!*

Creakle *Amamus, amatis, amant!*

Boys *Amamus, amatis, amant!*

David There never can have been a man who enjoyed his profession more
than Mr Creakle did.

Creakle *Imperfect!*

Boys *Amabam, amabas, amabat, amabamus, amabatis, amabunt!*

David When I think of him now — my blood rises against him — because
I know him to have been an incapable brute!

Creakle Future Perfect!

Boys (*lots of mistakes here*) *Amavero, amaveris, amaverit, amavermus,
amaveritis, amaverunt!*

David He had no more right to be possessed of that great trust he held than
to be Lord High Admiral, or Commander-in-Chief: in either of which
capacities, it is probable that he would have done *infinitely less mischief*!

SCENE 12

FRIENDS

The Lights dim. Night-time

We hear a strange tuneless tune on a flute

Young David is alone. David listens for a moment

Young David Mr Mell had a flute.

David My impression is, after many years of consideration, that there never
can have been anybody in the world who played worse.

The music stops. Mr Mell looks at Young David

Mr Mell The placard. Wretched. I'm sorry you've had such a beginning
here.

Young David Your shoe ——

Mr Mell Split. I know. No part of the original boot left. Rather poor. Paid
very little.
Young David I'm sorry. Would you like a cake? (*He offers him one*)
Mr Mell Kind. Thank you.
David He said little, but I think he liked me. And if I steadily picked up some
crumbs of knowledge — it was because of him. He had collected me from
the coach station, and on our way to the school we had visited his mother.
She was very poor indeed, and lived in an alms house. He never spoke of
her.
Young David Thank you for collecting me from the coach station. Please
tell your mother ——
Mr Mell (*momentarily alarmed*) SHH! Our secret ... (*A beat*) Good luck.
This is your bedroom.

And he shows him into a room where other boys are sleeping

Traddles (*stirring*) I say — here's a game. We have a dog to sleep with us.
Boy 2 Lie down, sir!
Boy 3 Good boy! Here, Towser — sit!
Boy 4 Sweet natured if you treat him right!
Boy 2 Creakle beware! We have a guard will savage you!
Boy 4 *Cave canem!*
Traddles You are welcome D. Copperfield, and may remove your placard.
You are among friends.
Young David Thank you.
Traddles I am Traddles T. We are a band of brothers, and have shed blood
together.

They recite their names and rallying cry

All Bucket — Bartle — Traddles — Socks: BLOOD BLOOD BLOOD!
Traddles But now it is time for you to meet our captain. Fellows! Carry this
hairy brute before Prince Hal.
Young David Who?
Traddles J. Steerforth: scholar, lover, poet, protector of the poor, glass of
fashion, et cetera.
Boy 2 Even Creakle is afraid of him.

*They carry Young David to Steerforth's door and bang on it. Another ritual
now*

The Lights come up on Steerforth

Boys *Dominus noster!*

Steerforth (*coolly*) *Quid est?*
Boys Bucket, Bartle — with Copperfield!
Steerforth Enter!

The boys deposit Young David in front of Steerforth, who is handsome, charming, sixteen or thereabouts. We hear some music that becomes associated with him and his influence. Older David is riveted and disconcerted by the sight of him. He talks to the audience while Young David talks to Steerforth. The other boys murmur their reactions

Steerforth Your story, Copperfield — a full account!
David Steerforth ——
Young David I had a new father ...
David — Steerforth became a person of great power in my eyes ——
Young David ... he was cruel to my mother ...
David — I felt proud to know him.
Young David ... sent away my nurse, my friend ...
David There was an ease in his manner — a kind of enchantment.
Young David ... frightened and checked us all...
David ... he carried a spell with him... a spell...
Young David ...locked out my mother... beat me...
David No veiled future glanced upon him in the moonbeams; none.
Young David ...and so I bit his hand, sir, and was sent away.
Steerforth It's a jolly shame!

The music fades. A beat, then admiring murmurs at the acceptance of the new boy. Young David is relieved, and smiles gratefully

Young David Why thank you, sir.
Steerforth Your stepfather sounds a rogue and a villain ... (*Beat*) What money have you got, Copperfield?
Young David Seven shillings.
Steerforth You had better give it to me to take care of. At least, you can if you like. You needn't if you don't like.
Young David Oh please! (*He gives it*)
Steerforth Do you want to spend anything now?
Young David No thank you.
Steerforth Perhaps you'd like to spend a couple of shillings or so, in a bottle of currant wine for tomorrow night ...
Young David Yes — I should like that.
Steerforth Very good. Some of it shall be kept to wet your whistle while you are story telling ...
Young David But what if Mr Creakle ——

Traddles On one boy alone has the dreaded Creakle never dared to lay a hand. That boy is J. Steerforth!

Steerforth I would like to see him try.

Young David What would you do if he did try?

Steerforth I would begin by knocking him down with a blow to the forehead from the seven and sixpenny ink bottle on the mantelpiece.

The boys are awestruck by this response

He is a fool. He knows less than any of us. All he understands is slashing. Especially Miss Traddles here.

Traddles It's true. Last term he beat me every day.

Steerforth Except the seventh Monday.

Traddles When he caned me on both hands. He used to be a hop dealer—

Steerforth But went bust.

Traddles Creakle is scared of Pegleg.

Steerforth Pegleg knows secrets about Creakle.

Traddles Secrets that could bring him down.

Steerforth Lock him up.

Traddles See him swing.

Young David But Mr Mell seems kind ...

Steerforth (*contemptuously*) Oh, Mr Mell!

Traddles Very poor.

Steerforth Old Mrs Mell — his mother — is as poor as Job.

Young David (*blurting*) Lives in an alms house on charity.

Steerforth Indeed?

Young David Oh dear ...

Traddles Just as we thought!

Steerforth He'd better watch himself.

Young David I didn't mean ——

Steerforth Now don't you worry, Copperfield. I'll take care of you. (*Calling out*) The rest of you — to sleep. (*To Young David*) My father died when I was young. I miss him. I'm sorry that you never knew your own.

Young David You're very kind. I am very much obliged to you.

Steerforth You haven't got a sister, have you?

Young David No.

Steerforth That's a pity. If you had had one, I should think she should have been a pretty, timid, little, bright-eyed sort of girl. I should have liked to know her. (*A beat*) Good-night, young Copperfield.

The Lights dim on the dormitory

SCENE 13

THE FIRST HALF

The boys tumble downstairs, and get to their places. Mr Mell scurries into position. Steerforth strolls to a chair

David And so — every night — we talked, and told stories and drank currant wine. The drawback was that often I felt sleepy or out of spirits at night ...
Young David And he helps me...
Steerforth *"Neque longius ab oceano"* — you see — "not further from the ocean than", and so forth.
Young David Thank you! (*To David*) My special friend.
David Yes, yes, how I admired and loved him.

Young David stands up to translate for Mr Mell. Creakle prowls

Young David (*translating*) And the point at which it flows into the Rhine is not more than sixty miles from the ocean ——
Mr Mell Eighty, Copperfield.
Creakle (*thwacking at him*) Eighty — Copperfield.
Steerforth Sorry, Copperfield.
Young David Ow.
Steerforth Be bold with him. I wouldn't have put up with that.
David But what about the Saturday when Steerforth insulted Mr Mell — in front of Creakle and the whole school?

SCENE 14

STEERFORTH V. MELL

Tension. Steerforth and Mr Mell confront one another. Creakle stares at them, the boys are silent, fascinated

Steerforth ... and then I called him a beggar. If *I* had been cool, perhaps I shouldn't have called him a beggar. But I did, and I am ready to take the consequences of it.

The boys are impressed by this speech

Creakle Your candour does you honour — but I am surprised, Steerforth, I must say, that you should attach such an epithet to any person employed and paid in Salem House, sir.

Steerforth Let him deny it.
Creakle Deny that he's a beggar, Steerforth?
Steerforth If he is not a beggar himself, his near relation's one. (*A beat*) His
mother lives on charity in an alms house.

Tension. All eyes on Mr Mell

Mr Mell (*looking at Young David, sighing*) Yes, I thought so.
Creakle Mr Mell. Have the goodness, if you please, to set him right before
the assembled school.
Mr Mell He is right, sir, without correction. What he has said is true.
Creakle Be so good then as to declare publicly, will you, whether it ever
came to my knowledge until this moment?
Mr Mell I believe not directly.
Creakle (*after a beat*) I believe you've been in a wrong position altogether,
and mistook this for a charity school. Mr Mell, we'll part if you please. The
sooner the better.
Mr Mell There is no time like the present.
Creakle Sir, to you.
Mr Mell I take my leave of you, Mr Creakle, and of all of you. James
Steerforth, the best wish I can leave you is that you may come to be
ashamed of what you have done today.

He turns, gathers up a few things, and leaves

A silence. Then cheers and celebrations. Young David looks wretched

Creakle and Tungay turn and follow Mr Mell

Day turns to night. We hear Mr Mell's flute

David (*to Young David*) How did I feel?
Young David Miserable.
David How did I feel that night?
Young David I thought I heard his flute …
David What did I think of Steerforth?
Young David He is very kind to me, and I don't know what I should ever
do here without him!
David Yes, yes. And Mr Mell?
Young David I soon forgot him.
David Then just before the holidays — Steerforth came to me.

Scene 15

So I Lost Her

Music under the following

Steerforth Davy? My dear fellow. Your mama.
Young David What of her?
Steerforth Creakle has a letter just this morning. (*A beat*) She's very ill.
Young David Oh.
Steerforth Very dangerously ill.

Young David is in tears

   (*Quietly*) She is dead.
David And so I lost her.

The music swells

   *Carriers bring on a coffin. A Clergyman, Murdstone and Peggotty are
   there*

Clergyman I am the resurrection and the light sayeth the Lord …

The funeral service and the music continue under the narration

   Barkis arrives during the following

David We stand around the grave. The day seems different to me from every
   other day, and the light not of the same colour — of a sadder colour.
Peggotty (*to Young David*) She was never well — for a long time. She was
   uncertain in her mind and not happy. The day you went away, she said to
   me: "I never shall see my pretty darling again. Something tells me so…"
   On the last night she said to me how kind and considerate your pa had
   always been to her, and that a loving heart was better and stronger than
   wisdom. "Lay your good arm under my neck," she said " and turn me to
   you, for your face is going far off and I want it to be near". Oh Davy, the
   time had come when my words to you were true — when she was glad to
   lay her poor head on her stupid cross old Peggotty's arm — and she died
   like a child that had gone to sleep.
David How did I think of her?
Young David As she was before!
David How did I remember her?

Young David As she was when it was just Mama and Peggotty and me.
David What did she look like?
Young David Pretty, and happy, and curling her hair round her finger, and
    dancing with me at twilight in the parlour …

*Music swells again. Peggotty is at one end of the coffin and Barkis at the
other. They stoop, take either end of the black funeral pall, and billow it up
into the air, scattering the mass of flower petals lying on it. They turn the pall
over. The reverse side is a great checked travelling rug. They lower it on to
the coffin, which is now the front bench of Barkis's cart*

SCENE 16

MRS BARKIS

*The noise of horses' hooves. Young David is squashed between Peggotty and
Barkis*

Young David It's a beautiful day, Mr Barkis.
Barkis It ain't bad.
Young David Peggotty is quite comfortable now, Mr Barkis.
Barkis Is she though? (*A beat*) *Are* you pretty comfortable?
Peggotty (*giggling*) I am I thank you, Mr Barkis!
Barkis (*sliding to her and beginning to squash Davy*) But really and truly,
    you know. Are you?
Peggotty Pretty comfortable — yes!
Barkis Are you? Really and truly pretty comfortable? Are you? Eh?
Peggotty (*yelping with laughter*) I am. *Yes I am*!
Barkis But *truly* ——
Peggotty You've squashed the poor baby into a pancake! Shift along, Mr
    Barkis.

Barkis chuckles and moves. Moments pass

Barkis But are you pretty comfortable though?

*Cries of outrage, delight; chuckles, etc. The shoving-up game is played
through the following narration*

David Mr Murdstone took the first opportunity to give Peggotty notice. She
    resolved to quit Blunderstone and seek her fortune at Yarmouth, where she
    could stay with her brother. She thought that I might go with her for a
    fortnight and Mr Murdstone gave his sour permission.

Barkis But truly though! Is you comfortable enough?
David By the time we got to Yarmouth — the breath was nearly wedged out
of my body.

Mr Peggotty and Ham sweep on to bid them welcome

*Bags and baskets are taken away during the following. First Peggotty helps,
and then Barkis*

Mr Peggotty Hoorroh! Mas'r Davy boy!
Ham Why how you have growed!
Young David Am I grown?
Ham Growed, Mas'r Davy bor'? Ain't he growed!
Mr Peggotty Ain't he growed!
Barkis (*aside to Young David*) I say — it was all right.
Young David Oh.
Barkis It didn't come to an end there. It was all right.
Young David Oh.
Barkis You know who was willin'. It was Barkis, and Barkis only. And it's
all right.

Barkis moves off with a basket

Mr Peggotty and Ham are there

Mr Peggotty We 'eard ——
Ham About your ma.
Mr Peggotty We 'eard ——
Ham And Little Em'ly cried an hour and more.
Mr Peggotty Another orphan, you see, sir. (*After a beat, to Ham with a
guffaw*) And here's another of 'em, though he don't look much like it!
Young David If I had you for my guardian, Mr Peggotty, I don't think I
should feel much like it!
Ham (*delighted*) Well said, Mas'r Davy bor'. Hoorah! Well said!

They move away with baskets, etc.

Young David Peggotty! Are you thinking of being married to Mr Barkis?
Peggotty (*flustered*) Why, what in heaven! Did I ever? Barkis — I never
heard the like — whatever can you — whatever ... Yes.
Young David It will be a very good thing. For then, you know, Peggotty, you
would always have the horse and cart to bring you over to see me, and could
come for nothing, and be sure of coming.

Peggotty (*with a shriek*) The sense of the dear! What I have been thinking of this month back!

Hugs and kisses galore

Emily comes on

David A figure appeared before long, and I soon knew it to be Em'ly, who was a little creature still in stature, though she was grown.
Young David Em'ly?
Emily Oh, it's you is it?
Young David You know who it is!
Emily And didn't you know who it was?

He makes to kiss her, she runs away

Mr Peggotty A little puss it is!
Ham So sh'is! So sh'is!!

They gather round in a noisy group

David When the term of my visit was nearly expired, it was given out that Peggotty and Mr Barkis were going to make a day's holiday together, and that Little Em'ly and I were to accompany them.

Loud goodbyes. The cart is off again. We never left it. Emily and David sit facing the audience, and Barkis and Peggotty sit facing upstage — the direction in which the cart is going

Away we went, and the first thing we did was to stop at a church.

Barkis and Peggotty disappear inside

Birds are singing. A pause

Young David (*making conversation*) My friend Steerforth would like it here in Yarmouth.
Emily And who is he?
Young David (*airily*) The head boy at the school I go to — went to. A close friend.
Emily An' what's he like?
Young David (*with immense enthusiasm*) Oh — handsome. And bold. Brave as a lion. And you can't think how frank he is. And he is astonishingly clever. And nothing seems to cost him any trouble. He

knows a task if he only looks at it. He is the best cricketer you ever saw. He will give you almost as many men as you like at draughts, and beat you easily!

Emily (*eyes sparkling*) I would like to see him.

Young David Oh he's such a generous, fine, noble fellow, that it's hardly possible to give him as much praise as he deserves. I can never feel thankful enough for the generosity with which he has protected me.

Emily It's a fine thing to have a gentleman protect you ...

Young David I shall protect you, Em'ly!

Emily (*giggling*) Thank you.

Young David I shall protect you because I love you and shall always love you!

Emily (*laughing*) You silly boy!

Young David I never could love anyone else, and I will kill any other man or boy who says they love you!

Emily And how will you do that? Perhaps you will ask your friend Mr Steerforth to help?

Young David Why — no ...

Emily laughs and laughs but kisses Young David — and lets him kiss her

Barkis and Peggotty return from church

Peggotty There! — like two young mavishes!

Barkis Left them for five minutes ...

Peggotty Turn our backs and look — it's courtin' time!

Barkis All aboard now!

Peggotty I'm starved! Dinner in half an hour.

Barkis Pork and greens! Pork and greens!

Peggotty We'll have us dinner at *The Willin' Mind*!

Barkis Mas'r Davy ...

Young David Yes?

Barkis You knows a lot for such a small'n ...

Young David Not so small, Mr Barkis.

Barkis I wager that you can't tell me what this woman's name might be ...

Young David Clara Peggotty, Mr Barkis.

Barkis No!

Young David Indeed it is, Mr Barkis!

A "No it ain't" "Yes it is" interchange can go on here if the director isn't worried about running times

Barkis Clara Peggotty *Barkis*!

Young David What?
Barkis Clara Peggotty Barkis!
Emily *Married!*
Peggotty We are, we are!
Young David (*amazed*) Why Peggotty!
Peggotty (*blushing and laughing*) I have thought of it night and day — every way I can, and I hope the right way, and I wouldn't so much as 'ave given it another thought if my Davy had been anyways against it.
Young David Look at me, Peggotty, and see if I am not really glad and don't truly wish it!

Hugs, celebrations, music — which melt into something gentle and calm. Day turns to night

During this, Peggotty and Barkis slowly stroll away, and Emily leaves

David Little Em'ly and I made a cloak of an old wrapper, and sat under it for the rest of the journey. Ah, how I loved her! What happiness if we were married, and were going away to live ——
Young David Never growing older, never growing wiser, children ever ——
David — rambling hand in hand through sunshine, laying down our heads on moss at night, and buried by the birds when we were dead.

By the end of the scene Young David is asleep

SCENE 17

THE WORLD OF ACTION

In the shadows, Quinion calls out. Young David wakes and looks about him

Quinion What, Brooks!
Young David No sir, David Copperfield.
Quinion You are Brooks of Sheffield — that's your name!
Young David No!
Quinion Where are you being educated, Brooks?

Murdstone emerges from the shadows

Murdstone He is not being educated anywhere at present. I don't know what to do with him.
Quinion The counting house, Murdstone.
Murdstone What of it?

Quinion We give employment to other boys. I see no reason why we
   shouldn't give employment to him.
Murdstone (*thoughtful*) Yes.
Quinion He having no other prospect.
Young David The counting house?
Murdstone Of Murdstone and Grinby, in the wine trade. This is a world for
   action, David, especially for a boy of your disposition — to which no
   greater service can be done than to force it to conform to the ways of the
   working world, and to bend it, and break it.

SCENE 18

MURDSTONE AND GRINBY'S

*The inhabitants of Murdstone and Grinby's Blackfriars warehouse take
over the stage. They shift crates of bottles, washing tub and Quinion's desk
into position. We hear the slurp of the river, and the damp drip drip of the
decaying, waterside building*

Quinion is present. During the following Micawber enters

Company 1 Murdstone and Grinby's warehouse was at the waterside.
Company 2 Down in Blackfriars.
Company 3 Behold its panelled rooms, discoloured with the dirt and smoke
   of a hundred years.
Company 1 Behold its decaying floors and staircase.
Company 3 The dirt and rottenness of the place.
Company 2 Listen for the squeaking and scuffling of the old grey rats in the
   cellar.
Quinion When the empty bottles run short, there are labels to be pasted on
   full ones — or corks to be fitted on them, or seals to be put upon the corks
   or bottles to be packed in cases.

Young David is in tears

David That I can have been so easily thrown away — a child of excellent
   abilities, with strong powers of observation: quick, eager, delicate; it seems
   wonderful to me that nobody should have made any sign on my behalf. I
   wanted so much ——
Young David — to know things. To be a person in the world …
David I felt ——
Young David — that nothing would ever change …

David I felt ——
Young David — ashamed.
David I became at ten years old, a little labouring hind in the service of Murdstone and Grinby!
Company At eight that evening, when the work was over…
Quinion (*gesturing at Young David*) This is he.
Micawber This, then, is Master Copperfield. I hope I see you well, sir?
Young David Very well, I thank you sir. And I hope you are too.
Micawber I am, thank heaven, quite well. I have received a letter from Mr Murdstone, in which he mentions that he would desire me to receive into an apartment in the rear of my house, which is at present unoccupied — and is, in short, to be let as a — in short — as a *bedroom* — the young beginner whom I now have the pleasure to ——
Quinion This is Mr Micawber.
Micawber Ahem! That is my name. My address is Windsor Terrace, City Road. I — in short — I live there.
Young David I'm afraid I don't know where Windsor Terrace is …
Micawber Under the impression that your peregrinations in this metropolis have not as yet been extensive, and that you might have some difficulty in penetrating the arcana of the modern Babylon — in short — that you might lose yourself, I have come in person, in order to install you in the knowledge of the nearest way!
Young David Oh thank you, thank you, sir!

SCENE 19

THE MICAWBERS

Music. Young David and Micawber set off

David Arriving at his house in Windsor Terrace — which I noticed was shabby like himself, but also, like himself, made all the show it could — he presented me to Mrs Micawber, who was sitting with a baby at her breast.

They arrive at Windsor Terrace

Mrs Micawber I never thought, before I was married when I lived with Papa and Mama, that I should ever find it necessary to take a lodger. But Mr Micawber being in difficulties, all considerations of private feeling must give way!
Young David Yes, ma'am.

Mrs Micawber Mr Micawber's difficulties are almost overwhelming just at present, and whether it is possible to bring him through them, I don't know. When I lived at home with Papa and Mama, I really should have hardly understood what the word meant — but experimentia does it — as Papa used to say ——

There is a sudden banging downstairs

Creditor (*off*) Oi! Oi you! Micawber!!
Micawber Death, humiliation and shame! My life is at an end! When will they leave me to crawl in peace and tatters to my grave!

The Micawbers are extremely agitated. Young David is baffled

Creditor (*off*) Come, Micawber! You ain't out yet, you know. Pay us, will you! Don't hide — you know that's mean. I wouldn't be mean if I was you. Pay us, will you? You just pay us, d'ya hear!
Mrs Micawber (*a dramatic announcement*) I shall swoon, I shall faint! I feel my blood draining to my feet! My head floats, my heart sinks, my legs give way. The world is fading! I can hardly see!
Creditor (*off*) Swindlers! Robbers and cheats! Swindling, thieving parasites! If I ever get my hands on you, Micawber, I'll twist your neck in such a knot …
Micawber Crushed! Crushed! Hope has sunk beneath the horizon. (*After a beat, noticing Young David*) Master Copperfield — could I perhaps prevail upon your young limbs to hurry down below and tell my old friend at the door that as we have company, I am — unhappily — not able to accommodate his request?

Young David hurries off to oblige

A few moments pass. The Micawbers listen intently

Creditor (*off; finally going*) And tell 'im — I'll be back!
Micawber (*after a beat*) Gone.
Mrs Micawber (*excited*) Gone.
Micawber The crisis has passed, my dear. Shall we eat?
Mrs Micawber With the exception of the heel of a Dutch cheese — which is not adapted to the wants of a young family — there is really not a scrap of anything in the larder.
Micawber Never fear! Something will turn up!

Young David returns

My very good friend! A young Horatius! We shall never forget your efforts
on our behalf, how can we ——

Mrs Micawber If Mr Micawber's creditors will *not* give him time, they must
take the consequences, and the sooner they bring it to an issue the better.
Blood cannot be obtained from a stone, neither can anything on account be
obtained at present from Mr Micawber!

Micawber A veal cutlet or lamb chops breaded. We shall venture out.

SCENE 20

THE SLOW AGONY OF YOUTH

Young David heads off through the London streets. Passers-by buffet him

David In this house, and with this family, I passed my leisure time. Mr
Micawber's difficulties were an addition to the distressed state of my mind
but in my forlorn mood I became quite attached to them all. But from
Monday morning until Saturday night, I worked at the warehouse.

Young David My salary ——

Quinion Six shillings a week.

Young David My food ——

Company 1 Stale pastry.

Company 2 Stout pale pudding.

Company 3 A slice of bread and butter.

Young David Half an hour for tea ——

Company 2 In Fleet Street.

Company 1 Or Covent Garden.

Company 3 Or lounging on old London Bridge.

Company 2 Are you all right?

Young David I'm very well, sir.

Company 1 You're pale as death.

Young David Only a little tired.

Company 3 Quite the little gent.

Young David Good-day, sir.

David From Monday morning until Saturday night ——

Company 1 No advice ——

Company 2 — no counsel ——

Company 3 — no encouragement ——

Company 2 — no consolation ——

Company 1 — no assistance ——

Company 4 — no support ——

Company 3 — of any kind ——

Young David — from anyone!
David (*asking Young David*) Did I ever think that I might be rescued?
Young David Never.
David Did I ever grow reconciled to any part of it?
Young David Never.
David And did I change?
Young David I feel a little shabby now...
David Was I unhappy?
Young David Yes.
David Who did I tell?
Young David No-one. Nobody.
David And was I lonely?
Young David All the time.
David (*in pain*) Lonely, secret, self reliant: the slow agony of my youth.
Micawber (*from another part of the stage*) Catastrophe!

SCENE 21

DEBTORS' PRISON

*The Lights shift. There is the sound of a door slam, locks locking, bolts
bolting. A shadow of prison windows*

Micawber Catastrophe ... Send for my knife and pint pot — both will be
   serviceable in the place to which I am bound, for the brief remainder of my
   life!
David At last Mr Micawber's difficulties came to a crisis, and he was
   arrested early one morning, and carried over to ——
Young David (*reading a sign*) The King's Bench prison in the Borough?
   (*Running to Micawber*) Mr Micawber...
Micawber Through these tears I conjure you: take warning from my fate.
   Annual income — twenty pounds, annual expenditure nineteen pounds,
   nineteen and six pence—result happiness. Annual income twenty pounds,
   annual expenditure twenty pounds ought and six, result misery. (*Elaborate
   tears and nose blowing. Then a sudden recovery*) Do you have by any
   chance a shilling with which I might purchase some two pints of porter?
   Here is an order drawn against Mrs Micawber for the sum.

*During the next speech, Mrs Micawber arrives in the prison room with
sundry belongings, and the tiny Micawber twins: two tightly-swaddled
babies. Young David goes to get the porter*

David Mrs Micawber resolved to move into the prison with the family and the remains of their furniture. Friends engaged to help them at their present pass, and they lived more comfortably in the prison than they had lived for a long time out of it.

Mrs Micawber My family have advised that Mr Micawber should apply for his release under the Insolvent Debtors Act. He will be free in six weeks!

Cheers and celebrations

Young David returns with the porter

Young David May I ask, ma'am, what you and Mr Micawber intend to do, when Mr Micawber is out of his difficulties, and at liberty?

Mrs Micawber My family are of the opinion that something might be done for a man of Mr Micawber's ability in the Custom House. The influence of my family being local, it is their wish that he should go down to Plymouth. They think it indispensable that he should be on the spot.

Young David That he may be ready?

Mrs Micawber Exactly — that he may be ready — in case of anything turning up.

Young David And do you go too, ma'am?

Mrs Micawber (*gradually becoming more and more hysterical*) I will never desert Mr Micawber. Mr Micawber may have concealed his difficulties from me in the first instance, but his sanguine temper may have led him to expect that he would overcome them. The pearl necklace and bracelets which I inherited from Mama have been disposed of for less than half their value; and the set of coral, which was the wedding gift of my papa, has been actually thrown away *for nothing* …

Micawber (*nervously*) Emma …

Mrs Micawber But I never will desert Mr Micawber. No! I never will do it! It's of no use asking me!

Micawber Emma, dearest Emma …

Mrs Micawber (*beside herself*) Mr Micawber has his faults. I do not deny that he is improvident. I do not deny that he has kept me in the dark as to his resources and his liabilities, both, — but I never — will — desert — Mr — Micawber!

Micawber (*holding her down*) Emma, my angel!

Mrs Micawber I never will desert you, Micawber!!

Micawber My life! I am perfectly aware of it.

Mrs Micawber He is the parent of my children! He is the father of my twins! He is the husband of my affections — and I never will desert Mr Micawber!

Micawber Be calm!

Mrs Micawber *No!*

Micawber I beseech you — look up!
Mrs Micawber *No, no!*
Micawber Ah this has been a dreadful day! We stand alone now —
everything is gone from us!
Young David But surely …

Scene 22

Stranded!

Micawber helps Mrs Micawber from the room. Young David is left alone

David Mr and Mrs Micawber were so used to their old difficulties, I think
that they felt quite shipwrecked when they came to consider that they were
released from them. But I ——
Young David Going away!
David What to do? What to do?

Aunt Betsey enters during the following

Young David Nobody! There will be nobody.
David A new lodging …
Young David Unknown people. Turned adrift …
David I recognized a voice I'd never heard myself ——
Aunt Betsey Mrs David Copperfield, I *think.*
Young David (*faintly*) Yes.
Aunt Betsey (*slight bow*) Miss Trotwood. You have heard of her I dare say?
Young David (*with growing enthusiasm*) Yes.

Scene 23

Good Advice

The Lights change

*The Micawbers and their children are aloft on some representation of a stage
coach. Music under the following*

Mrs Micawber I shall never forget you. Your conduct has always been of
the most delicate and obliging description. You have never been a lodger.
You have been a friend.

Micawber My dear young friend — I am older than you; a man of some experience in life, and — and of some experience, in short, in difficulties, generally speaking. Until something turns up — which I am, I may say, hourly expecting — I have nothing to bestow but advice, and my advice is this. Never do tomorrow what you can do today. Procrastination is the thief of time. Collar him!

The Coachman is ideally seen in a cape and hat, clutching a post-horn

Coachman All aboard for the Plymouth Coach!
Mrs Micawber Master Copperfield, God bless you! I never can forget your help, you know, and I never would if I could.

Farewells, hankies waved, the sound of the post-horn, and the coach departs

Scene 24

Escape!

Young David I have resolved to *run away*!

Aunt Betsey is on another part of the stage

Young David is remembering

Aunt Betsey Miss Trotwood. You have heard of her I dare say?
Young David My mother told me of her!
Aunt Betsey Why, bless my heart! You are a very baby.
Young David She cannot be so terrible. She thought Mama a baby. She is kind if she is stern. She will help me.
Aunt Betsey Have some tea!
Young David She lives near Dover. I do not know exactly where ... But I have saved a few shillings for the journey!

A Thief is suddenly next to him

Thief I'll help you with your bags.
Young David Why, thank you.
Thief Give 'em here.
Young David Yes, yes.
Thief And sixpence.
Young David (*getting his money*) Yes, let me see ...

The Thief grabs it all

Thief What's this! *What's this!* This is a pollis case, is it? You're going to
bolt, are you? Come to the pollis!
Young David You give me my money back if you please, and leave me
alone!
Thief Come to the pollis! You shall prove it yourn to the pollis!
Young David Give me my bags and money, will you!
Thief Away with you!

The Thief knocks Young David over and heads off with bags and money

Young David NO! *No!*

*A chase, up and around. The sound of shouts, squeals, cart wheels, running
feet, etc.*

Company 1 Ran after him.
Company 2 No breath to call out with.
Company 3 Lost him.
Company 4 Saw him.
Company 3 Lost him!
Company 2 Cut at with a whip.
Company 3 Shouted at!
Company 1 Down in the mud.
Company 4 Up again!
Company 3 Running into somebody's arms.
Company 2 Running headlong at a post!
Company 1 Confused by fright and heat!
Company 4 Left the young man to go where he would.
Company 3 Faced about for Greenwich!
Company 2 On the Dover Road.
Young David Can't go back, can't go back.
David Trudged on.
Company 3 Past a little shop where clothes were bought.

Dolloby is at a counter

Dolloby (*suspicious*) The name's Dolloby!
Young David My waistcoat — I am to sell it for a fair price …
Dolloby What's a fair price?
Young David Eighteen pence?
Dolloby Ninepence.
Young David Ninepence!?

Dolloby Ninepence.
Company 2 And set off again, richer by ninepence.
Company 4 Climbed out at last upon Blackheath.
Company 3 Slept beneath the stars.
Young David And the next day, got through three and twenty miles on the
   straight road.
Company 1 Slept again.
Company 2 Walked into Chatham.

A Mad Old Man, a sudden terrifying apparition

Mad Old Man *What do you want?* Oh my eyes and limbs, what do you want?
   Oh my lungs and liver, what do you want?
Young David Would you buy a jacket?
Mad Old Man Oh let's see the jacket; oh my heart on fire, show the jacket
   to us! Oh my eyes and limbs, oh goroo — how much for the jacket?
Young David Half a crown!
Mad Old Man Oh my lungs and liver — *no!* Oh my eyes, *no!* Oh my limbs,
   no! Eighteen pence. Goroo!
Young David I'll take eighteen pence ——
Mad Old Man Don't ask for money! Get out of my shop! Don't ask for
   money!

The Mad Old Man runs into the shop and hides

Young David My money! Give me my money!
Mad Old Man Will you go for sixpence!
Young David I can't! I shall be starved!
Mad Old Man Will you go for a shilling …?
Young David I want the money badly …
David (*on his way again*) And settled for a shilling.
Company 2 And limped seven miles upon the road.
David And came at last to Dover!
Young David Excuse me sir, I'm looking for my Aunt. Betsey Trotwood.
   Do you know her?
Company 3 The Betsey Trotwood — nah, she's made fast to the great buoy
   outside the harbour. You can't reach her till half-tide.
Company 1 Last seen in Friday's gale — on a broomstick — heading for
   Calais.
David But at last ——

Janet appears

Janet My mistress — what do you want with her, boy?

Young David To speak to her, if you please.
Janet To beg of her, you mean.
Young David No. (*A beat. Of course, that's exactly what he has in mind*)
  That is …
Janet This is Miss Trotwood's. Now you know; and that's all I have got to
  say.

SCENE 25

AUNT BETSEY GETS A SHOCK

A pretty country garden

*Suddenly Aunt Betsey erupts from her house: a handkerchief madly tied in
her hair, wearing gardening gloves and a gardener's apron, et cetera*

Aunt Betsey Go away! Go along! No boys here!
Young David If you please, ma'am ——
Aunt Betsey I said — no boys.
Young David If you please, Aunt.
Aunt Betsey I said … (*Thunderstruck*) Eh?
Young David If you please, Aunt, I am your nephew.
Aunt Betsey (*collapsing*) Oh, Lord!
Young David I am David Copperfield of Blunderstone in Suffolk — where
  you came on the night I was born and saw my dear mama. I have been very
  unhappy since she died. I have been slighted and taught nothing, and
  thrown upon myself, and put to work not fit for me. It made me run away
  to you. I was robbed at first setting out, and have walked all the way, and
  have never slept in a bed since I began the journey. (*Tears. He falls to the
  ground*)
Aunt Betsey Mercy on us! Stop — sit up. Mercy on us! Stop it! No call for
  tears — shan't listen — ear-muffs. Mercy on us! What's the matter with
  him? Janet! *Janet!*

*Young David is struck silent by the force of these "Janets". Aunt Betsey is
instantly more composed*

  Janet arrives

  Go upstairs — give my compliments to Mr Dick, and say I wish to speak
  to him.

  Janet goes

  I suppose you think Mr Dick a short name?

Young David (*reading*) And Charles the First will not allow the treatment of his subject Dick ——

The music stops

Aunt Betsey Franklin used to fly a kite. He was a quaker, or something of that sort, if I am not mistaken. And a quaker flying a kite is a much more ridiculous object than anybody else!

David Some days passed. Then ——

Aunt Betsey (*shouting*) Donkeys!

SCENE 27

MURDSTONE VANQUISHED

Aunt Betsey charges out in pursuit of trespassing donkeys. Many a shriek and yell. Much braying

Mr Dick hides behind a chair

Aunt Betsey returns, belabouring the head of Mr Murdstone

Aunt Betsey Go along with you! You have no business here! How dare you trespass!

Murdstone Madam! Restrain yourself!

Aunt Betsey Don't "madam" me! Impertinent trespasser! Donkey-driver! Invader!

Young David (*terrified*) This is Mr Murdstone, Aunt.

Aunt Betsey I don't care who it is! He comes on donkey's back to trespass! I won't allow it! Go away! Janet, turn him round. Lead him off! (*A beat*) Who did you say?

Murdstone Mr Edward Murdstone.

Aunt Betsey Ah. I was not aware at first to whom I had the pleasure of objecting. Hmph. Sit down, sit down.

Murdstone Miss Trotwood ——

Aunt Betsey The same Murdstone who married the mother of this boy?

Murdstone I am.

Aunt Betsey I think it would have been a much better and happier thing if you had left that poor girl alone.

Murdstone (*trying to ignore this*) Miss Trotwood — on the receipt of your letter, I considered it an act of greater justice to myself, and perhaps of more respect to you ——

Young David I ——

Aunt Betsey He's got a longer name — Babley — Mr Richard Babley — but don't you call him by it. He can't bear his name. That's a peculiarity of his.

Mr Dick, grey hair on end, appears behind Aunt Betsey and is winking and giggling at Young David

He has been ill-used enough, by some that bear it, to have a mortal antipathy to it, Heaven knows … (*Seeing Mr Dick*) Mr Dick! — Don't be a fool, because nobody can be more discreet than you can, when you choose. Now. You have heard me mention David Copperfield. Now don't pretend not to have a memory, because you and I know better.

Mr Dick (*blankly*) David Copperfield? Oh yes — to be sure, David Copperfield.

Aunt Betsey He has done a pretty piece of business — he has run away. Ah! His sister Betsey Trotwood never would have run away ——

Young David (*astonished*) My sister?

Aunt Betsey (*impatiently*) The girl you should have been! The girl I came to see!

Mr Dick (*completely lost*) You think she wouldn't have run away?

Aunt Betsey Bless and save the man, how he talks! Don't I know she wouldn't? She would have lived with me and we would have been devoted to one another. But here you see young David Copperfield, and the question I put to you is this. What shall we do with him?

Mr Dick (*vaguely*) What indeed … yes … what shall we do with him?

Aunt Betsey Yes — I want some very sound advice.

Mr Dick Why, if I were you … If I were you — I should — er … (*Sudden inspiration, a leap, a cry of delight*) I should *wash* him.

Aunt Betsey Janet — Mr Dick sets us all right. Heat the bath!

Janet exits to heat the bath

(*Suddenly screaming*) Janet! Donkeys!

Loud braying. And she runs to the end of the garden path and starts belabouring a donkey that has strayed on to her patch. This could be a mime or there could be some representation of the donkey

Meanwhile, Young David changes into "a pair of giant trousers, a big old shirt and three shawls"

David (*shouting*) I don't know — whether my aunt — had any lawful right of way — over the little piece of green — in front of the house — but the one great outrage of her life — was the passage of a donkey — over that immaculate spot!

Aunt Betsey (*triumphant*) Donkeys!

David The bath was a great comfort, and we dined soon after I awoke, off a roast fowl and a pudding.

Young David, now strangely dressed, approaches

(*Observing Young David*) I felt not unlike a trussed bird myself. I told her my story. When I had finished, they burnt my old clothes.

Quick pause. Music

That night I stood at the window of my room.

Young David Look at the moonlight on the sea.

David I seemed to float down the melancholy glory of that track upon the water — away into the world of dreams …

A moment. The music fades. Loud calls of "good-morning" as the house wakes up

SCENE 26

MR DICK

David The next day ——

Aunt Betsey I have written to him.

Young David To ——?

Aunt Betsey To Murderer — *Murdstone* — I have sent him a letter that I'll trouble him to attend to, or he and I will fall out, I can tell him!

Young David Shall — I — be — given up to him?

Aunt Betsey I don't know. We shall see.

Young David I can't think what I shall do if I have to go back to Mr Murdstone.

Aunt Betsey I don't know anything about it! We shall see.

Young David But ——

Aunt Betsey Mr Dick! Bid good-morning to the boy!

Mr Dick (*laughing merrily*) Ah! Phoebus! How does the world go? I tell you what — I shouldn't wish it to be mentioned, but it's a — it's a mad world!

Aunt Betsey How goes the Memorial, Dick?

Mr Dick I believe I have made a start. I think I have made a start. You have been to school?

Young David Yes sir, for a short time.

Mr Dick Do you recollect the date when King Charles the First had his head cut off?

Young David 1649 — I think.

Mr Dick Well, so the books say. But I don't see how that can be. Because, if it was so long ago, how could the people about him have made that mistake of putting some of the trouble out of *his* head, after it was taken off, into *mine*?

Young David Er …

Mr Dick It's very strange.

Aunt Betsey Fetch your kite, Dick, and show David.

Mr Dick goes

What do you think of him? Come — your sister Betsey Trotwood would have told me what she thought of anyone, directly. Be as like your sister as you can, and speak out!

Young David Is he — is Mr Dick — I ask because I don't know, Aunt — is he at all out of his mind, then?

Aunt Betsey Not a morsel!

Young David Oh, indeed.

Aunt Betsey If there is anything in the world that Mr Dick is not, it's that.

Young David Oh indeed.

Aunt Betsey He has been *called* mad — and nice people they were, who had the audacity to call him mad. If it hadn't been for me, his own brother would have shut him up for life. I stepped in. He is the most friendly and amenable creature in existence!

Young David And Charles the First ——

Aunt Betsey Ah yes. King Charles. Mr Dick's allegorical way. He connects his illness with great disturbance and agitation, naturally. That's the figure he chooses to use. Of course — it interferes with his memorial — the petition he's writing to the Lord somebody-or-other about his affairs. But it don't signify — it keeps him amused. Shhhh!

Mr Dick returns, carrying a seven-foot kite made out of closely written manuscript

A gentle moment. Distant music through the the following

Mr Dick I made it. We'll go and fly it, you and I.

Aunt Betsey Made with pieces of his very own memorial.

Aunt Betsey Oh stuff. You needn't mind me.

Murdstone — to answer it in person. This unhappy boy has been the
occasion of much domestic trouble and uneasiness; both during the
lifetime of my late dear wife, and since. He has a sullen, rebellious spirit;
a violent temper, and an untoward, intractable disposition ——

Aunt Betsey Strong!

Murdstone But not at all too strong for the facts.

Aunt Betsey Ha! (*A beat*) Well, sir?

Murdstone I have my own opinions as to the best mode of bringing him up,
and placed the boy under the eye of a friend of mine in a respectable
business ——

Aunt Betsey If he had been your own boy, you would have sent him there,
just the same, I suppose? But now — what have you got to say next?

Murdstone Merely this, Miss Trotwood. I am here to take David back, to
dispose of him as I think proper, and to deal with him as I think right. You
may have some idea of abetting him in his running away. But I must caution
you that if you step in between him and me, now, you must step in, Miss
Trotwood, for ever.

Aunt Betsey And what does the boy say? Are you ready to go, David?

Young David (*nervously at first*) No. *No.* Please — I don't want to go. Mr
Murdstone has never liked me, or been kind to me. He made my mother
unhappy about me. He *made* her so. I know it. Peggotty knows it. Please
— *please*, Aunt Betsey — for my father's sake — take me in. Don't give
me back to him!

Aunt Betsey Mr Dick!

Mr Dick jumps with alarm

What shall we do with this child?

Mr Dick is blank

Mr Dick (*suddenly inspired*) Have him measured for a suit of clothes
directly!

Aunt Betsey Mr Dick — give me your hand, for your common sense is
invaluable. (*To Murdstone*) You can go when you like; I'll take my chance
with the boy. If he's all you say he is, at least I can do as much for him then,
as you have done. But I don't believe a word of it.

Murdstone Miss Trotwood — if you were a gentleman ——

Aunt Betsey Bah! Stuff and nonsense! Don't talk to me! Do you think I don't
know what kind of life you must have led his poor, unhappy, mother? Do
you think I don't know what a woeful day it was for the soft little creature,
when you first came in her way, smirking and making great eyes at her!

Murdstone This is either insanity or intoxication ——

Aunt Betsey Mr Murdstone — you were a tyrant to the simple baby, and you broke her heart. She was a loving baby — and through the best part of her weakness, you gave her the wounds she died of. And this poor child you sometimes tormented her through is a disagreeable remembrance and makes the sight of him odious now. Ay, ay! You needn't wince, I know it's true without that.

A long moment, Murdstone breathing heavily, "as if he had been running"

Good-day, sir! And goodbye! And let me see you ride a donkey over my green again, and as sure as you have a head upon your shoulders, I'll knock your hat off, and tread upon it too!

Murdstone stares at her — furious, then turns on his heel and goes

Mr Dick waves a cheery goodbye. A beat

Aunt Betsey He could have crushed us all three, and fed us to the seagulls!

Young David *Bravo*, Aunt! *Bravo*, Mr Dick!

Mr Dick Who was he exactly?

Young David And I don't ever have to go back there?

Aunt Betsey Not while Betsey Trotwood is above ground you won't!

Young David (*hugging his protectors*) Thank you, thank you, thank you! Aunt Betsey — I won't ever forget. I won't ever let you down. I won't —

Aunt Betsey (*delighted*) You won't carry on in such a fashion — or I'll know the reason why! Mr Dick — you'll consider yourself guardian, jointly with me, of this child.

Mr Dick I shall be delighted!

Aunt Betsey Very good — that's settled. I have been thinking — do you know, Mr Dick, that I might call him Trotwood. Trotwood Copperfield!

Mr Dick To be sure. Yes yes — to be sure! Trotwood Copperfield!!

Aunt Betsey I give you — Master Trotwood Copperfield!

Aunt Betsey		Master Trotwood Copperfield!
Young David	} (*together*) {	Master Trotwood Copperfield?
Mr Dick		Master Trotfield Copperwood — er— Master Trotwood Copperspoon — er…

And they go

SCENE 28

THE CATHEDRAL SCHOOL

David Thus I began my new life, in a new name, with new clothes, and very
   soon — in a new school.

*The rest of the cast start to sing the Cathedral School Song. It's a classic
Victorian affair: organ and sturdy voices. See music notes on page viii*

Company   Oh sun-drenched cloisters, ancient school
                   Whose pride is book and pen;
                   Where honour, faith and learning rule
                   Where trust is discipline's best tool
                   And boys turn into men!

Aunt Betsey leads Young David into Wickfield's study

Aunt Betsey Trotwood! This is Mr Wickfield. He's my man of business —
   looks after money for ladies too busy to look after it themselves — and
   looks after it very well. Wickfield — this is my nephew.
Wickfield Wasn't aware you had one, Miss Trotwood.
Aunt Betsey I have adopted him, and I have brought him here, to put him
   to a school where he may be thoroughly well taught, and well treated. Now
   tell me where that school is, and what it is, and all about it.
Wickfield Here in Canterbury?
Aunt Betsey Certainly.
Wickfield At the best we have, your nephew couldn't board just now ... But
   I'll tell you what you can do, Miss Trotwood. Let him stay here with us and
   attend school daily. This is a capital house for study. As quiet as a
   monastery and almost as roomy. Leave him here!
Aunt Betsey I am very much obliged to you!
Wickfield Then you must meet my little housekeeper.

And Agnes arrives

Wickfield Here she is. My joy. My daughter Agnes. She does not go to
   school. Miss Trotwood — let us discuss arrangements.

Wickfield and Aunt Betsey withdraw

Young David You've never been to school?
Agnes Oh yes! Every day.

Young David You mean here — in your home?

Agnes Papa couldn't spare me to go anywhere else. His housekeeper must be in his house you know.

Young David He is very fond of you I am sure.

Agnes Yes. (*A beat*) Mama has been dead ever since I was born. I only know her picture, in the hall. I saw you looking at it. Did you think whose it was?

Young David Yes — it is very like you.

Agnes You are very welcome, Trotwood!

And another chorus breaks out

During the following, Agnes goes and Wickfield returns

Company   Cathedral school! Beloved nest!
                     Our wings you test, our wings you fledge!
                     For thee we will give up our rest
                     Renounce the worst, attain the best
                     To you, our hearts we pledge!

Firelight. Wickfield is a little drunk. Young David sits by him

Wickfield Should you like to stay with us, Trotwood, or to go elsewhere?

Young David To stay!

Wickfield You are sure?

Young David If you please. If I may!

Wickfield Why, it's but a dull life that we lead here I'm afraid.

Young David No more dull for me than Agnes, sir. Not dull at all!

Wickfield Than Agnes. Than Agnes! (*A beat*) Now I wonder whether my Agnes tires of me. When should I ever tire of her. I must keep her near me … If it is miserable to bear this life when she is here, what would it be and she away? No, no, no … I can not try that.

An awkward moment. Young David gets up

Good-night, sir.

Young David leaves Mr Wickfield

The Lights change. Uriah Heep calls to him from the shadows

Heep Master Copperfield?

Young David Yes?

Heep Uriah Heep.

Young David Good-day. (*A beat*) I suppose you are another great lawyer?

Heep Me, Master Copperfield? Oh no! I'm a very 'umble person. I am well aware that I am the 'umblest person going, let the other be where he may. My mother is likewise a very 'umble person. We live in an 'umble abode, Master Copperfield, but have much to be thankful for. My father's former calling was 'umble. He was a sexton.

Young David What is he now?

Heep He is a partaker of glory at present, Master Copperfield, but we have much to be thankful for. How much do I have to be thankful for, in living with Mr Wickfield, whose kind intention is to give me my articles, which would otherwise not lay within the 'umble means of mother and self!

Young David Perhaps you'll be a partner in Mr Wickfield's business one of these days, and it will be Wickfield and Heep, or Heep late Wickfield.

Heep Oh no, Master Copperfield — I am much too 'umble for that!

Young David My aunt ——

Heep Your aunt is a sweet lady. She has a great admiration for Miss Agnes, Master Copperfield, I believe?

Young David Yes.

Heep I hope you have too, Master Copperfield, but I am sure you must have.

Young David Everybody must have.

Heep Oh thank you, Master Copperfield for that remark! It is so true! 'Umble as I am, I know it is so true! Oh thank you Master Copperfield! (*After a beat, prying*) I suppose you'll stop here some time, Master Copperfield?

Young David As long as I remain at the school.

Heep Oh indeed! I should think you would come into the business at last, Master Copperfield.

Young David I never thought of it. Good-night, Mr Heep.

And Young David goes

But Uriah keeps calling after him — gurgling and giggling a little to himself, but ending nastily

Heep Oh, yes, Master Copperfield, I should think you would indeed! Oh indeed Master Copperfield, I should think you would certainly! Yes, yes, Master Copperfield, without question. Yes, Master Copperfield, you're just the type. Yes — yes ...

Wickfield approaches with Dora. Young David returns, but Older David appears. Wickfield addresses him now

Wickfield Copperfield, may I introduce Miss Dora Spenlow. Her aunts have brought her down for a few days in the country. They are her guardians.

Wickfield goes

David sees Dora and gasps. Young David runs between them. They cannot see or hear him. Music

David Miss Spenlow…
Young David Pretty ——
David Dora.
Young David Pretty and happy.
David What a beautiful name!
Young David Curling her hair round her finger.
David Would you … Could you … Might I … ?
Dora I should be delighted!
Young David And dancing with me at twilight in the parlour.

And David dances with Dora. Young David watches, amazed, then goes and dances with her as he did with his mother

David (*watching her*) She was more than human to me. She was anything that no-one ever saw, and everything that everybody ever wanted. I was swallowed up by love — no looking down, no looking back.

And the three dance together as the Lights fade and the music swells

CURTAIN

Young David I ——

Aunt Betsey He's got a longer name — Babley — Mr Richard Babley — but don't you call him by it. He can't bear his name. That's a peculiarity of his.

Mr Dick, grey hair on end, appears behind Aunt Betsey and is winking and giggling at Young David

He has been ill-used enough, by some that bear it, to have a mortal antipathy to it, Heaven knows … (*Seeing Mr Dick*) Mr Dick! — Don't be a fool, because nobody can be more discreet than you can, when you choose. Now. You have heard me mention David Copperfield. Now don't pretend not to have a memory, because you and I know better.

Mr Dick (*blankly*) David Copperfield? Oh yes — to be sure, David Copperfield.

Aunt Betsey He has done a pretty piece of business — he has run away. Ah! His sister Betsey Trotwood never would have run away ——

Young David (*astonished*) My sister?

Aunt Betsey (*impatiently*) The girl you should have been! The girl I came to see!

Mr Dick (*completely lost*) You think she wouldn't have run away?

Aunt Betsey Bless and save the man, how he talks! Don't I know she wouldn't? She would have lived with me and we would have been devoted to one another. But here you see young David Copperfield, and the question I put to you is this. What shall we do with him?

Mr Dick (*vaguely*) What indeed … yes … what shall we do with him?

Aunt Betsey Yes — I want some very sound advice.

Mr Dick Why, if I were you … If I were you — I should — er … (*Sudden inspiration, a leap, a cry of delight*) I should *wash* him.

Aunt Betsey Janet — Mr Dick sets us all right. Heat the bath!

Janet exits to heat the bath

(*Suddenly screaming*) Janet! Donkeys!

Loud braying. And she runs to the end of the garden path and starts belabouring a donkey that has strayed on to her patch. This could be a mime or there could be some representation of the donkey

Meanwhile, Young David changes into "a pair of giant trousers, a big old shirt and three shawls"

David (*shouting*) I don't know — whether my aunt — had any lawful right
of way — over the little piece of green — in front of the house — but the
one great outrage of her life — was the passage of a donkey — over that
immaculate spot!
Aunt Betsey (*triumphant*) Donkeys!
David The bath was a great comfort, and we dined soon after I awoke, off
a roast fowl and a pudding.

Young David, now strangely dressed, approaches

(*Observing Young David*) I felt not unlike a trussed bird myself. I told her
my story. When I had finished, they burnt my old clothes.

Quick pause. Music

That night I stood at the window of my room.
Young David Look at the moonlight on the sea.
David I seemed to float down the melancholy glory of that track upon the
water — away into the world of dreams …

*A moment. The music fades. Loud calls of "good-morning" as the house
wakes up*

SCENE 26

MR DICK

David The next day ——
Aunt Betsey I have written to him.
Young David To ——?
Aunt Betsey To Murderer — *Murdstone* — I have sent him a letter that I'll
trouble him to attend to, or he and I will fall out, I can tell him!
Young David Shall — I — be — given up to him?
Aunt Betsey I don't know. We shall see.
Young David I can't think what I shall do if I have to go back to Mr
Murdstone.
Aunt Betsey I don't know anything about it! We shall see.
Young David But ——
Aunt Betsey Mr Dick! Bid good-morning to the boy!
Mr Dick (*laughing merrily*) Ah! Phoebus! How does the world go? I tell you
what — I shouldn't wish it to be mentioned, but it's a — it's a mad world!
Aunt Betsey How goes the Memorial, Dick?

Young David You mean here — in your home?

Agnes Papa couldn't spare me to go anywhere else. His housekeeper must be in his house you know.

Young David He is very fond of you I am sure.

Agnes Yes. (*A beat*) Mama has been dead ever since I was born. I only know her picture, in the hall. I saw you looking at it. Did you think whose it was?

Young David Yes — it is very like you.

Agnes You are very welcome, Trotwood!

And another chorus breaks out

During the following, Agnes goes and Wickfield returns

Company   Cathedral school! Beloved nest!
                     Our wings you test, our wings you fledge!
                     For thee we will give up our rest
                     Renounce the worst, attain the best
                     To you, our hearts we pledge!

Firelight. Wickfield is a little drunk. Young David sits by him

Wickfield Should you like to stay with us, Trotwood, or to go elsewhere?

Young David To stay!

Wickfield You are sure?

Young David If you please. If I may!

Wickfield Why, it's but a dull life that we lead here I'm afraid.

Young David No more dull for me than Agnes, sir. Not dull at all!

Wickfield Than Agnes. Than Agnes! (*A beat*) Now I wonder whether my Agnes tires of me. When should I ever tire of her. I must keep her near me … If it is miserable to bear this life when she is here, what would it be and she away? No, no, no … I can not try that.

An awkward moment. Young David gets up

   Good-night, sir.

Young David leaves Mr Wickfield

The Lights change. Uriah Heep calls to him from the shadows

Heep Master Copperfield?

Young David Yes?

Heep Uriah Heep.

SCENE 28

THE CATHEDRAL SCHOOL

David Thus I began my new life, in a new name, with new clothes, and very
soon — in a new school.

The rest of the cast start to sing the Cathedral School Song. It's a classic
Victorian affair: organ and sturdy voices. See music notes on page viii

Company   Oh sun-drenched cloisters, ancient school
                     Whose pride is book and pen;
                     Where honour, faith and learning rule
                     Where trust is discipline's best tool
                     And boys turn into men!

Aunt Betsey leads Young David into Wickfield's study

Aunt Betsey Trotwood! This is Mr Wickfield. He's my man of business —
looks after money for ladies too busy to look after it themselves — and
looks after it very well. Wickfield — this is my nephew.
Wickfield Wasn't aware you had one, Miss Trotwood.
Aunt Betsey I have adopted him, and I have brought him here, to put him
to a school where he may be thoroughly well taught, and well treated. Now
tell me where that school is, and what it is, and all about it.
Wickfield Here in Canterbury?
Aunt Betsey Certainly.
Wickfield At the best we have, your nephew couldn't board just now ... But
I'll tell you what you can do, Miss Trotwood. Let him stay here with us and
attend school daily. This is a capital house for study. As quiet as a
monastery and almost as roomy. Leave him here!
Aunt Betsey I am very much obliged to you!
Wickfield Then you must meet my little housekeeper.

And Agnes arrives

Wickfield Here she is. My joy. My daughter Agnes. She does not go to
school. Miss Trotwood — let us discuss arrangements.

Wickfield and Aunt Betsey withdraw

Young David You've never been to school?
Agnes Oh yes! Every day.

Murdstone This is either insanity or intoxication ——

Aunt Betsey Mr Murdstone — you were a tyrant to the simple baby, and you broke her heart. She was a loving baby — and through the best part of her weakness, you gave her the wounds she died of. And this poor child you sometimes tormented her through is a disagreeable remembrance and makes the sight of him odious now. Ay, ay! You needn't wince, I know it's true without that.

A long moment, Murdstone breathing heavily, "as if he had been running"

Good-day, sir! And goodbye! And let me see you ride a donkey over my green again, and as sure as you have a head upon your shoulders, I'll knock your hat off, and tread upon it too!

Murdstone stares at her — furious, then turns on his heel and goes

Mr Dick waves a cheery goodbye. A beat

Aunt Betsey He could have crushed us all three, and fed us to the seagulls!

Young David *Bravo*, Aunt! *Bravo*, Mr Dick!

Mr Dick Who was he exactly?

Young David And I don't ever have to go back there?

Aunt Betsey Not while Betsey Trotwood is above ground you won't!

Young David (*hugging his protectors*) Thank you, thank you, thank you! Aunt Betsey — I won't ever forget. I won't ever let you down. I won't —

Aunt Betsey (*delighted*) You won't carry on in such a fashion — or I'll know the reason why! Mr Dick — you'll consider yourself guardian, jointly with me, of this child.

Mr Dick I shall be delighted!

Aunt Betsey Very good — that's settled. I have been thinking — do you know, Mr Dick, that I might call him Trotwood. Trotwood Copperfield!

Mr Dick To be sure. Yes yes — to be sure! Trotwood Copperfield!!

Aunt Betsey I give you — Master Trotwood Copperfield!

Aunt Betsey   Master Trotwood Copperfield!

Young David ⎫   ⎧ Master Trotwood Copperfield?

Mr Dick   ⎬ (*together*) ⎨ Master Trotfield Copperwood — er — Master

               ⎭   ⎩ Trotwood Copperspoon — er...

And they go

Aunt Betsey Oh stuff. You needn't mind me.

Murdstone — to answer it in person. This unhappy boy has been the occasion of much domestic trouble and uneasiness; both during the lifetime of my late dear wife, and since. He has a sullen, rebellious spirit; a violent temper, and an untoward, intractable disposition ——

Aunt Betsey Strong!

Murdstone But not at all too strong for the facts.

Aunt Betsey Ha! (*A beat*) Well, sir?

Murdstone I have my own opinions as to the best mode of bringing him up, and placed the boy under the eye of a friend of mine in a respectable business ——

Aunt Betsey If he had been your own boy, you would have sent him there, just the same, I suppose? But now — what have you got to say next?

Murdstone Merely this, Miss Trotwood. I am here to take David back, to dispose of him as I think proper, and to deal with him as I think right. You may have some idea of abetting him in his running away. But I must caution you that if you step in between him and me, now, you must step in, Miss Trotwood, for ever.

Aunt Betsey And what does the boy say? Are you ready to go, David?

Young David (*nervously at first*) No. *No*. Please — I don't want to go. Mr Murdstone has never liked me, or been kind to me. He made my mother unhappy about me. He *made* her so. I know it. Peggotty knows it. Please — *please*, Aunt Betsey — for my father's sake — take me in. Don't give me back to him!

Aunt Betsey Mr Dick!

Mr Dick jumps with alarm

What shall we do with this child?

Mr Dick is blank

Mr Dick (*suddenly inspired*) Have him measured for a suit of clothes directly!

Aunt Betsey Mr Dick — give me your hand, for your common sense is invaluable. (*To Murdstone*) You can go when you like; I'll take my chance with the boy. If he's all you say he is, at least I can do as much for him then, as you have done. But I don't believe a word of it.

Murdstone Miss Trotwood — if you were a gentleman ——

Aunt Betsey Bah! Stuff and nonsense! Don't talk to me! Do you think I don't know what kind of life you must have led his poor, unhappy, mother? Do you think I don't know what a woeful day it was for the soft little creature, when you first came in her way, smirking and making great eyes at her!

Mr Dick I believe I have made a start. I think I have made a start. You have been to school?

Young David Yes sir, for a short time.

Mr Dick Do you recollect the date when King Charles the First had his head cut off?

Young David 1649 — I think.

Mr Dick Well, so the books say. But I don't see how that can be. Because, if it was so long ago, how could the people about him have made that mistake of putting some of the trouble out of *his* head, after it was taken off, into *mine*?

Young David Er …

Mr Dick It's very strange.

Aunt Betsey Fetch your kite, Dick, and show David.

Mr Dick goes

What do you think of him? Come — your sister Betsey Trotwood would have told me what she thought of anyone, directly. Be as like your sister as you can, and speak out!

Young David Is he — is Mr Dick — I ask because I don't know, Aunt — is he at all out of his mind, then?

Aunt Betsey Not a morsel!

Young David Oh, indeed.

Aunt Betsey If there is anything in the world that Mr Dick is not, it's that.

Young David Oh indeed.

Aunt Betsey He has been *called* mad — and nice people they were, who had the audacity to call him mad. If it hadn't been for me, his own brother would have shut him up for life. I stepped in. He is the most friendly and amenable creature in existence!

Young David And Charles the First ——

Aunt Betsey Ah yes. King Charles. Mr Dick's allegorical way. He connects his illness with great disturbance and agitation, naturally. That's the figure he chooses to use. Of course — it interferes with his memorial — the petition he's writing to the Lord somebody-or-other about his affairs. But it don't signify — it keeps him amused. Shhhh!

Mr Dick returns, carrying a seven-foot kite made out of closely written manuscript

A gentle moment. Distant music through the the following

Mr Dick I made it. We'll go and fly it, you and I.

Aunt Betsey Made with pieces of his very own memorial.

Young David (*reading*) And Charles the First will not allow the treatment of his subject Dick ——

The music stops

Aunt Betsey Franklin used to fly a kite. He was a quaker, or something of that sort, if I am not mistaken. And a quaker flying a kite is a much more ridiculous object than anybody else!
David Some days passed. Then ——
Aunt Betsey (*shouting*) Donkeys!

SCENE 27

MURDSTONE VANQUISHED

Aunt Betsey charges out in pursuit of trespassing donkeys. Many a shriek and yell. Much braying

Mr Dick hides behind a chair

Aunt Betsey returns, belabouring the head of Mr Murdstone

Aunt Betsey Go along with you! You have no business here! How dare you trespass!
Murdstone Madam! Restrain yourself!
Aunt Betsey Don't "madam" me! Impertinent trespasser! Donkey-driver! Invader!
Young David (*terrified*) This is Mr Murdstone, Aunt.
Aunt Betsey I don't care who it is! He comes on donkey's back to trespass! I won't allow it! Go away! Janet, turn him round. Lead him off! (*A beat*) Who did you say?
Murdstone Mr Edward Murdstone.
Aunt Betsey Ah. I was not aware at first to whom I had the pleasure of objecting. Hmph. Sit down, sit down.
Murdstone Miss Trotwood ——
Aunt Betsey The same Murdstone who married the mother of this boy?
Murdstone I am.
Aunt Betsey I think it would have been a much better and happier thing if you had left that poor girl alone.
Murdstone (*trying to ignore this*) Miss Trotwood — on the receipt of your letter, I considered it an act of greater justice to myself, and perhaps of more respect to you ——

ACT II

Scene 1

Steerforth Again

Some brisk, celebratory music, and a light bangs up on David

David ENGAGED!

The company cheer from off stage

But for how long!? (*A beat*) My dearest, darling Dora!

Dora appears

Dora Dearest silly boy!

David I have loved you every minute, night and day since I first saw you. No lover has ever loved, might, could, would, or should ever love, as I love you!!

Dora I have been painting flowers. Those dear things you brought me from Covent Garden. They are so — so very — so very, very ——

David How long will it be before your aunts let us marry? At dinner last night — I dined off the sight of you entirely, and sent away half a dozen plates untouched!

Dora I thought the food delightful — or are you teasing me …

David (*indicating one that he is wearing*) I have bought four sumptuous waistcoats, not for myself — I have no pride in them. For you!

Dora I am concerned that you expect me to wear waistcoats. Is it the fashion?

David My aunt has settled that I go to Yarmouth for a fortnight, while we think about my future.

Dora My aunts are sending me to Paris for a month. Do the ladies wear waistcoats there?

David I stay a night in London, then take the coach tomorrow.

Company London!

Dora goes

The Lights cross-fade to an area where there are chairs and tables with tablecloths

Steerforth is sitting at one table. A waiter lurks

Steerforth My God! It's little Copperfield!

David (*ridiculously pleased, going to Steerforth*) Steerforth? I never, never, never was so glad! My dear Steerforth, I am overjoyed to see you! (*He is in tears*)

Steerforth (*a hint of mockery at David's tears*) Now Copperfield old boy, don't be so overpowered!

David (*blushing, lying*) Onions — dust.

Steerforth But how do you come to be here?

David I came from Canterbury, today. I have been adopted by an aunt in that part of the country, and have just finished my education there. At the Cathedral School. I've been there seven years, I ——

Steerforth I am what they call an Oxford man — that is to say I get bored to death down there periodically. I'm on my way to my mother's, but I stopped to see the opera.

David I have been there too — at Covent Garden. What a delightful and magnificent entertainment!

Steerforth My dear young Davy — you are a very daisy. The daisy of the field at sunrise is not fresher than you are! I have been at Covent Garden too, and there never was a more miserable business. But I should like to hear what you are doing, and where you are going, and all about you. I feel as if you were my property.

David I am due to stay a fortnight with my old nurse in Yarmouth, I ——

Steerforth So you are in no hurry then! Come home with me to Highgate and stay a day or two. You will be pleased with my mother — she is a little vain and prosy about me, but that you can forgive her — and she will be pleased with you.

David She has every reason to be proud of you. You'll take a high degree at college, Steerforth, if you have not done so already.

Steerforth I take a degree! Not I! My dear Daisy — will you mind my calling you Daisy?

David Not at all!

Steerforth That's a good fellow! My dear Daisy, I have not the least desire or intention to distinguish myself in that way. Why should I trouble myself that a parcel of heavy-handed fellows may gape and applaud? Let them do it to some other man. There's fame for him, and he's welcome to it. (*A beat*) It's late. Good-night, dear Daisy. I shall call for you tomorrow. Good-night.

Steerforth goes

A light comes up on Young David

Young David My friend Steerforth would like it here in Yarmouth.
David And who is he?
Young David The head boy at the school I go to — went to ...
David (*troubled, quiet*) And what's he like?
Young David Oh — handsome and bold — brave as a lion. And you can't
think how frank he is.

Young David turns to watch David

David I am particular about this man because he made a particular effect on
me at that time, and because of what happened later ...
Micawber (*off*) My dear Copperfield!
David A dashing way he had of treating me like a plaything ...
Micawber My dear young Copperfield ...
David Young — young ...

SCENE 2

MICAWBER AND HEEP

Micawber arrives

Micawber This is indeed a meeting which is calculated to impress the mind
with a sense of the instability and uncertainty of all human — in short it is
a most extraordinary meeting!
David Mr Micawber!
Micawber Walking along the street, discussing with a new and valued
companion the probability of something turning up, I find an old and
valued friend turn up, who is connected with the most eventful period of
my life! Copperfield, my dear fellow, how do you do.
David I am glad to see you. And Mrs Micawber?
Micawber Thank you. She is tolerably convalescent. The twins no longer
derive their sustenance from nature's founts — in short — they are
weaned!
David And are you ... have you ... do you ... ?
Micawber There have been periods of my life when it has been requisite that
I should pause, that I should fall back, before making what I trust I shall not
be accused of presumption in terming — a spring. You find me at the
present — fallen back for a spring; and I have every reason to believe that
a vigorous leap will shortly be the result.
David You spoke of a companion. Will you not invite him to join us?

Micawber He lurks like Phoebus in the clouds of dawn. Come forth and
shine upon us! And perhaps we can prevail upon Mr Copperfield to join
us in a pint of port.

Uriah Heep emerges from the shadows

David is astonished

Heep Why, Master — I should say, Mister — Copperfield! How proud I am
to once again enjoy your company.
David Uriah!
Micawber You are acquainted! Is Copperfield in truth a friend of yours,
Heep?
Heep I am too 'umble sir, to call myself the *friend* of Master — I should say
Mister Copperfield. Mr Wickfield — of whom I have spoken — lodged
Master Copperfield in his house while Master Copperfield went from
strength to triumph at his school. He has been a patron to us both.
David And how is Mr Wickfield, Uriah?
Heep A good and worthy man, Master Copperfield. I bless the day he
stooped to bring me through his door.
David Is he in health?
Heep You know — of course — you know too well, Master Copperfield,
how it is with him.
David He drinks a little ...
Heep There — you've noticed too! What did I tell you, Mr Micawber?
David I——
Micawber Let us go through and talk. Heep — be our vanguard.

Micawber and Heep go

The scene begins to change

*A liveried flunkey removes tablecloths to reveal the elegant tables of an
upper class household*

David (*to the audience*) It surprised and made me uneasy to see Mr
Micawber and Uriah Heep arm-in-arm.

Steerforth comes forward

Steerforth Daisy!
David But all thought of this was wiped from my mind by the journey I made
with Steerforth the following day — to Highgate!

SCENE 3

HIGHGATE

Mrs Steerforth and Rosa Dartle glide on

In the background, someone is playing Schubert on the piano. The impression is one of rich, claustrophobic luxury

Steerforth Copperfield — my mother!

Mrs Steerforth It was at Mr Creakle's, my son tells me, that you first became acquainted.

David He was very generous and noble to me in those days, ma'am. I should have been quite crushed without him.

Mrs Steerforth He is always generous and noble.

David (*fervently*) Yes indeed!

Steerforth Rosa — this is David Copperfield. Daisy — Miss Dartle.

David and Rosa speak the following to each other as in the third person

David She had a scar upon her lip ——

Rosa It was an old scar, and healed years ago.

David It cut through her mouth, downward towards her chin. It was scarcely visible ——

Rosa Except above and on her upper lip, the shape of which it altered.

Steerforth (*to David*) We are distantly related. She is my mother's companion.

David Good-evening.

Rosa But really, Mr Copperfield, is Daisy a nick-name? And why does he give it you? Is it — eh? — because he thinks you young and innocent? I am so stupid in these things.

David (*blushing*) I think so.

Rosa Oh! Now I am glad to know that! I ask for information, and I am glad to know it. He thinks you young and innocent; and so you are his friend. Well, that's quite delightful.

The Lights change to suggest a passage of time

David (*to the audience*) After dinner, I sat with Mrs Steerforth over tea, while Rosa played at backgammon with James.

Mrs Steerforth My son tells me you were quite devoted to him, and that when you met yesterday, you made yourself known to him with tears of joy. I am not surprised at my son's inspiring such emotions, but I can assure you that he feels an unusual friendship for you, and that you may rely upon his protection.

Steerforth He shall not have it for much longer. Dear Daisy has resolved to visit his old nurse in Yarmouth, and will soon desert us!

David How happy I should be if you would only go there with me!

During the following, Mr Peggotty, Peggotty, Emily and Ham appear amongst the Steerforth tribe and form a tableau

You would meet her family! You would be delighted to see that household.

Steerforth Should I? Well — I think I should. It would be worth a journey — not to mention the pleasure of a journey with you, Daisy, to see that sort of people together, and to make one of 'em!

The Peggotty group have invaded the scene. They are invisible to David, Steerforth and his family. The Lights alter to suggest Yarmouth

Ham Two year, two year I waited — like you said. And she come to me now! Look here! Look here! This is to be my little wife!

Everyone holds their breath

Emily (*after a beat*) Yes, Uncle — if you please.

Mr Peggotty (*a roar of delight and congratulation*) If I please? Lord, as if I should do anythink else! Do you hear? Do you hear? Yes — Uncle — if you please! And do you think what 'twas you said — two year ago?

Peggotty (*mimicking*) "What him? — *Him* that I've known so intimate so many years! Oh Uncle! I can never have him! He's such a good fellow ..."

Much laughter

Emily (*after the laughter has subsided*) If you please, I am steadier now, and I have thought better of it, and I'll be as good a little wife as I can to him, for he's a dear, good fellow ...

They kiss. The Peggoty family and Emily move to the Boathouse

The Lights shift the focus back to Highgate

Rosa Oh but really? Do tell me. Are they, though?

Steerforth Are they what? And are who what?

Rosa "That sort of people." Are they really animals and clods, and beings of another order? I want to know *so* much.

Steerforth (*unclear if Rosa is serious*) They are wonderfully virtuous, I dare say, but they have not very fine natures, and they may be thankful that, like their coarse, rough skins, they are not easily wounded.

Rosa Really! Well it's such a delight to know that, when they suffer, they don't feel!

Aware of a certain tension, Mrs Steerforth rises

Sometimes I have been quite uneasy for that sort of people; but now I shall just dismiss the idea of them altogether.

Mrs Steerforth moves to go

Live and learn. I don't know, and now I do know; and that shows the advantage of asking — don't it?

Rosa withdraws with Mrs Steerforth

David She is very clever, is she not?
Steerforth Clever! She brings everything to a grindstone and sharpens it. She has worn herself away by constant sharpening. She is all edge.
David What a remarkable scar that is upon her lip.
Steerforth Why, the fact is — I did that.
David An accident?
Steerforth No. I was young and she exasperated me. I threw a hammer at her. A promising young angel I must have been. (*A beat*) She will bear the mark to her grave — if she ever rests in one, though I hardly believe she will ever rest anywhere.

SCENE 4

THE ASTONISHED FAMILY

The moment is held. Then the focus shifts and the Lights change

Mrs Steerforth and Rosa go

Steerforth and David acquire coats

We catch a glimpse of Dora

David Dearest Dora, I write to you from Yarmouth!
Dora Dearest Doady — I have learnt the most delightful song from Monsieur Boulot. It goes: "Ta ra la, ta ra la, ta ra la Ta; Fa ra la, Ta ra la, Fa la ra, Ha!"

David We came down by the Mail. I was very much concerned for the honour of Yarmouth, so that when my friend Steerforth said ——

Steerforth It seems a good, queer, out-of-the-way kind of hole.

David — I was highly pleased.

Dora goes

Steerforth and David are at the door of the boathouse. A burst of noise and chatter

Mr Peggotty Mas'r Davy! It's Mas'r Davy!

Peggotty (*with a scream*) My darling boy!

As David speaks the others interrupt, asking him how he is, etc.

David Peggotty! I am very glad to see you, very glad! Mr Peggotty! But, Peggotty — where is Mr Barkis?

Peggotty Oh — bad abed with the rheumatics — but the sight of you'll do him more good than pints of liniment!

David Why, Ham — how well you look! And Em'ly. This is my dear friend — my dear friend Steerforth!

Steerforth David has told me so much about you — I feel that we know each other of old.

Mr Peggotty Bravely said, bravely said.

Peggotty Davey has written us about you. Bless you, bless you for your kindness to him.

Mr Peggotty Em'ly my darlin' — come here! (*To Steerforth, indicating Ham*) This man sir, my brother's boy — not much of a person to look at — rough — a good deal o' the sou'wester in him — wery salt — but an honest sort of a chap, what does this blessed tarpaulin go and do? He offers his heart to Little Em'ly, and today, sir, today — that little girl says "yes, Uncle, if you please" — she says yes to him. Yes!

Steerforth Mr Peggotty — you are a thoroughly good man, and deserve to be as happy as you are tonight. My hand upon it!

Others (*adlib*) Hooroar! Congratulations! Heartiest congratulations! That ever I should live … My little nephy …

Ham She warn't no higher than you was, Mas'r Davy — when you first come. I see her grow up — gentl'men — like a flower. I'd lay down my life for her — Mas'r Davy — Oh! most content and cheerful! She's more to me, gentl'men, than — she's all to me that ever I can want, and more than ever I — than ever I could say …

Steerforth Ham — I give you joy, my boy. My hand upon that too! Sit down by me! And Mr Peggotty — unless you can induce your gentle niece to come and sit here too, I shall go.

Mr Peggotty Come, my darlin', don't you be shy now.

Emily moves to sit by Steerforth and not by Ham

Steerforth Thank you. Now I feel that this is my home. Thank you indeed!
Mr Peggotty, your house — a Lowestoft Ketch on my life! — the mizen
mast lowered through here, for a hammock pole!
Mr Peggotty Yes, yes — God bless my soul — it's true.

*During the following, Mr Peggotty begins to sing from "Ye Mariners of
England" and Steerforth joins in with the next line. They sing it beautifully*

David (*to the audience*) He filled the room like light and air. There was no
noise, no effort, no consciousness in anything he did. He brought us by
degrees into a charmed circle.

David speaks to Emily, who turns from the charmed circle to look at him

Young David And would you like to be a lady?
Emily (*softly*) Oh yes I should like it very much. We would all be gentlefolks
together then. We wouldn't mind when there come stormy weather.
David Yes.

The singing stops

Emily (*to the room*) Oh I should like to go in a coach and four, and sail upon
the sea, and pick a flower in every country of the world and bring them back
for Uncle Dan!
Steerforth And so you shall, and so you must!
Ham If we should find us treasure in the sand, we might!
Emily Why shouldn't we? We might be better than we are, we might do
better than we do! The poor men drowned, the poor girls sewing for a penny
… Children see a ship out yonder, doen't know how it got there, where it
come from.

And suddenly Emily bursts into tears

Ham Doen't, Em'ly! Doen't, my dear. Poor little tender heart.
Emily (*crying and smiling*) Oh Ham! I am not as good a girl as I ought to be!
I try your love too much. I'm often cross and changeable, when I should
think of nothing but how to make you happy.
Ham I am happy in the sight of you.

Emily It might have been a better fortune for you, if you had been fond of
someone else — someone steadier and worthier who was all bound up in
you — and never vain and changeable like me …

*During the next speech, the Yarmouth folk go and people arrive and dress
David and Steerforth in coats and hand them travelling bags*

SCENE 5

CHUCKLE HEADS

Dora is on another part of the stage

David My dearest and most loving Dora! I am jealous of the very streets in
Paris — that see you every day.
Dora Strange to report — I really do believe they think in French.
David Peggotty and all her family were full of grief at our going. We
departed to the regret and admiration of all concerned.

The Lights fade on Dora

We are back at Highgate. Schubert piano music

Rosa is present, with Steerforth and David

Rosa (*quizzically*) Two weeks.
Steerforth Well. What a quaint place, and what quaint company! It's been
a new sensation to mix with them.
David I never saw people so happy.
Steerforth A chuckle-headed fellow for the girl, isn't he?
Rosa What girl is that? A relation of Mr Copperfield's? I only ask because
it is better to know than not to know.
Steerforth No. On the contrary — Mr Copperfield used to have a great
admiration for her.
Rosa Why, hasn't he now? Is he fickle?
David No! She is as virtuous as she is pretty. She is engaged to be married
to her cousin, a most worthy and deserving man.
Steerforth (*winking at David*) If it were not that I might appear to disparage
her intended, which I know dear Daisy would not like, I would add that to
me she seems to be throwing herself away; that I am sure she might do
better, and that I swear she was born to be a lady.

SCENE 6

DAVID'S FUTURE

The Lights cross to Aunt Betsey on another part of the stage

Aunt Betsey Trotwood!

Steerforth and Rosa leave

David A letter from my aunt summoned me to the Adelphi.
Aunt Betsey There is a furnished little set of chambers to be let here, Trot, which ought to suit you to a marvel!
David (*arriving to inspect them*) Oh Aunt! This is the very thing! They are so ——
Aunt Betsey Cramped.
David Compact — neat.
Aunt Betsey Now, Trot — the future. What I want you to be is a firm fellow. A fine, firm fellow with a will of your own. With resolution. With determination. With strength of character that is not to be influenced, except on good reason, by anybody, or anything. What will you do with your life? Agnes tells me that you fancy yourself in love.
David Fancy, Aunt! I love Dora with my whole soul.
Aunt Betsey Dora, indeed! And you mean to say the little thing is very fascinating, I suppose?
David Aunt ——
Aunt Betsey And not silly?
David Silly, Aunt!
Aunt Betsey Not light-headed?
David (*maybe it's true*) Light-headed!
Aunt Betsey Well, well! I only ask. I don't depreciate her. Poor little couple! And so you think you were formed for one another, and are to go through a party-supper-table kind of life, like two pretty pieces of confectionery, do you?
David We love one another truly! If I ever thought Dora could love anybody else — or that I could love anybody else ...
Aunt Betsey Ah Trot! Blind, blind, blind! (*A beat*) Look for earnestness. Deep, downright, faithful, earnestness. (*A beat*) But now — I must be going. If ever there was a donkey trespassing on my green, there was one this afternoon at four o'clock. A cold feeling came over me from head to foot. (*A beat*)

Aunt Betsey hurries off

Clocks tick. Distant bells ring

David And so I was established in chambers in Buckingham Street in the
Adelphi. I lived principally on Dora and coffee ... But there were times
when it was very dreary. I wanted someone to talk to. I missed Agnes.
Agnes. Who had been my constant companion at Canterbury — the
repository of all my confidence. But within a week ——

SCENE 7

MY FIRST DISSIPATION

There is a mighty hammering on the door

*Steerforth bursts in. He is a little drunk: restless, bleak, cavalier. He is
accompanied by Traddles*

David Steerforth!
Steerforth See what I picked up in the street below!
David (*looking at Traddles*) I'm sorry, I ——
Traddles School. Salem House. (*A beat*) Traddles T.
David Traddles! Traddles my dear fellow — I am delighted to see you.
Steerforth Why Daisy, what a rare old bachelor you are here.
Traddles Delighted — delighted!
David But what have you ... where have you ... ?
Steerforth I shall make a town house of this place, unless you give me notice
to quit.
David If you wait for that, you will wait till doomsday!
Traddles Reading for the bar ——
Steerforth Miss Traddles is to be a lawyer!
Traddles Three others and myself unite to have a set of chambers ——
Steerforth Dear Daisy — we shall bless you with a housewarming — this
very night, then you shall be my guests at some dry party where I have to
visit for an hour.
Traddles I have the fourth of a room, and the fourth of a clerk ——
Steerforth Traddles!
Traddles We quarter the clerk you see. Half a crown a week he costs me!
Steerforth *Traddles!* Dust yourself down, disturb the world a little; take this
guinea to the wine shop down below, see what you can get with it. And
bring the bottles opened.
David And here are glasses waiting.

Traddles (*being bundled out*) I earn a little from a publisher, as a compiler
— on an Encyclopaedia ——

Traddles goes

Steerforth As soft as ever!

David Good hearted.

Steerforth (*tense*) Daisy, Daisy, Daisy! I detest this mongrel time — neither
day nor night ...

David Steerforth, what's the matter?

Steerforth I have been thinking that all the people that have made us
welcome, all those people who we found so glad on that first night in
Yarmouth, might — while we sweat in this great, wasted city — be
dispersed, or dead, or... (*A beat*) David. I wish to God I had had a judicious
father these last twenty years!

David What on earth ... ?

Steerforth I wish with all my soul I could guide myself better!

David What has caused this? Steerforth — I cannot hope to advise, but I may
at least sympathize with you.

Steerforth (*coming to, laughing a little*) Tut, it's nothing, Daisy! Nothing!
I am heavy company for myself sometimes. Confounding myself as the
bad boy "who didn't care", and became food for lions. What old women
call the horrors have been creeping over me from head to foot. I have been
afraid of myself.

David You are afraid of nothing else, I think.

Steerforth Well! So it goes by. So much for that. "being gone, I am a man
again" like Macbeth.

Traddles returns

Traddles Here! Six bottles of the best they had.

Steerforth You know — I went to Yarmouth once again ...

David (*incredulous*) This last week?

Steerforth (*grabbing two bottles and pouring wine into the glasses*) Two
apiece. We shall warm ourselves, Miss Traddles!

David What an extraordinary fellow you are, Steerforth!

Steerforth I have bought a boat down there.

Traddles There is some change, a shilling and odd pennies ——

Steerforth A clipper. Mr Peggotty will be master of her in my absence.

Traddles More change than I have in my pocket of a Monday!

David Now I understand you, Steerforth! What you have done is to confer
a benefit on him! Your generosity ... !

Steerforth (*sharply*) *No!* No… The less said, the better. We have said
enough.

A beat. They drink

David And what is she called?
Steerforth What!?
David The boat.
Steerforth Oh. Yes indeed. She's the *Stormy Petrel* now, but I'll have her
christened again.
David By what name?
Steerforth The *Little Emily!*
David A toast! The *Little Emily* — the ship and her patron!
Traddles (*enthusiastic*) Whoever they may be! I drink to them!
David The *Little Emily!*

A long drink. Laughter, gasps. Steerforth starts to sing "Annabel Lee"

*The three men move off to the party, which opens up in another part of the
stage*

SCENE 8

DRUNK

David Began, cheerful and light hearted — held forth on all sorts of matters
— laughed at my own jokes … We'll have a party like this once a week!
Went out into the night — foggy, frosty …
Traddles (*not as drunk*) You all right, Copperfield?
David Neverberrer! The party — arrived — bright lights — ladies, music …

We hear the booming noise of a party

Agnes is with Mr Wickfield and just behind them Uriah Heep

Whole room … looks as though it's learning to swim!… Can't get a hold
of it … better dance … try to dance … Charming lady! — will you perhaps
… could you consider … I ——

They come up against Agnes

David Agnes! Lorblessmer! Agnes!

Agnes (*embarrassed*) Hush! pray! You disturb the company. Sit down.
David Mr Wick — and Heep ... Wickfield and Heep, Wickfield and Heep ...
Agnes (*upset by this*) Please, Trotwood ...
Heep Could I oblige you, Miss Wickfield, by supporting Mr Copperfield to
    another room?
David Whasthis? Agnes ... I'mefraidyou'renorwell ...
Heep How distressing for you, Miss Wickfield.
David Nothankyouriah, no thankyou ...
Agnes Trotwood!

David collapses. The noise of the party reaches crescendo. Traddles and
Heep gather David up and carry him to a couch. Steerforth dances a step or
two with Agnes, but she quickly disengages herself

    Steerforth pushes past Traddles and goes

SCENE 9

AGNES

Traddles, Heep and Wickfield are at a distance

Evidence of coats and people waiting. Some hours have passed

David stirs on the couch

Agnes (*gently*) Trotwood?
David Oh what a stupid, stupid fool. Oh. Oh my head, oh my eyes. Oh my!
Agnes Mr Traddles will take you to his lodgings for the night. Uriah will help.
David (*remorseful*) If it were anyone but you, Agnes — I should not mind
    it half so much. I almost wish I were dead ...
Agnes Sshh! Don't be unhappy, Trotwood. If you cannot confidently trust
    me, whom will you trust?
David You are my good angel.
Agnes No.
David Indeed you are!
Agnes Well, if that is so...
David Yes?
Agnes Then let me warn you against your bad angel.
David (*after a moment*) If you mean Steerforth ——
Agnes I do.
David Then Agnes — you wrong him very much. It is unjust to judge him
    on what you saw tonight.

Agnes You have made a dangerous friend …

Heep comes towards them

Heep Are you feeling better Master Copperfield — I beg your pardon —
Mister Copperfield, but the other comes so natural. I don't like that you
should put a constraint upon yourself, but Mr Traddles is waiting, and I
fear, Miss Agnes, that your good father is very tired. He and I have much
to do tomorrow.
Agnes Of course. One minute, Mr Heep.

Heep retreats

(*Hushed*) He is going to enter into partnership with Papa.
David (*shocked*) Uriah? That mean, conniving … You must prevent it!
Agnes It was forced upon Papa ——
David By whom?
Agnes By Uriah. He is subtle, watchful. He has mastered Papa's weaknesses,
fostered them, taken advantage of them. (*In tears*) His ascendancy over
Papa is very great.
David Pray Agnes, don't! Don't, my dear sister…

Heep and Wickfield start to approach Agnes

Heep No need to be anxious, Mr Wickfield. I have the papers.
Wickfield My copies. Did I bring them with me?
Heep You'll make Miss Agnes fret to see you carry on this way.
Wickfield Of course. Of course. It's late — I'm tired.
Heep It would be a happiness for me to call a little later for you in the
morning.
Wickfield You're very kind.
Heep If you would only sign these papers now.
Wickfield You have them here?
Heep Of course.
Wickfield Nothing important.
Heep Nothing important. Expenses, business charges, deficiencies.
Wickfield Did we not clear a pile of these last week?
Heep A backlog had accumulated.
Wickfield (*strained*) What would I do without you? I hardly know which
way to turn.
Heep To me, Mr Wickfield, always to me. Your 'umble servant. And yours,
Miss Agnes. And now yours, Master Copperfield.

Agnes Thank you, Uriah. I shall see my father to our lodgings. Trotwood! (*Aside*) Be friendly to Uriah, don't repel him. Think first of Papa and me.

Agnes goes with Wickfield

Heep (*watching them go*) Mr Wickfield, a worthy man — but how imprudent he has been.
David Imprudent, Mr Heep?
Heep Very imprudent indeed, Master Copperfield — But I wish you'd call me Uriah. Like old times at Canterbury.
David Uriah, then.
Heep Thank you! Thank you, Master Copperfield. It's like the blowing of old breezes or the ringing of old bellses to hear *you* say Uriah. Yes, yes. But Mr Wickfield. Well. If anyone else had been in my place during the last few years, by this time he would have had Mr Wickfield under his thumb. (*Slowly, acting it out*) Un — der — his — thumb. (*A beat*) Of course — I have Miss Agnes to consider.
David (*sharply*) What's that, Uriah?
Heep Oh how pleasant to be called Uriah, spontaneously! But, Mr Copperfield, I have a confidence that I wish to take the liberty of reposing. 'Umble as I am — the image of Miss Agnes has been in my breast for years. Oh Master Copperfield, with what a pure affection do I love the ground my Agnes walks on.
David (*dazed, horrified, hung over*) What!
Heep (*not so nice*) And you're quite a dangerous rival, Master Copperfield. You always was, you know ...
David Do you suppose that I regard Miss Wickfield otherwise than as a very dear sister?
Heep You may not, you know. But then, you see, you may!
David Well then — I will tell you — I am engaged to another young lady. I hope that contents you.
Traddles My dear fellow — my heartiest congratulations.
Heep How glad, how very glad I am that you have had the condescension to return my confidence. Now — If you'll have the goodness to keep my secret, and not in general to go against me, I shall take it as a particular favour. My Agnes is very young still. I shall have time gradually to make her familiar with my hopes, as opportunities offer. (*A beat*) Dear me, it's past one. And I have to arrange business with Mr Wickfield in the morning. Good-night, Master Copperfield. My 'umble, grateful thanks.

Heep goes

A moment's hush

David (*staggering to his feet*) Rogue! Villain! Rascal! Give me the bottle,
  Traddles, give it to me! I'll after him and break it over his confounded head!
  Agnes and this creature! He is the very devil!
Traddles Not immediately likeable, I grant you. But clever I'll be bound.
David (*subsiding*) Monster!
Traddles (*cheerfully*) I'm not clever at all. A plodding sort of fellow — good
  at stating cases, making abstracts, but I have no invention, not a particle.
  I swear — there never was a fellow with less originality than I have.

SCENE 10

VISIONS

*Agnes appears with Wickfield and Heep, as though at a wedding. The
Micawbers walk forward*

David I fell into a doze. The image of Agnes and her father rose before me
  and filled me with vague terrors ——
Agnes Have you met my husband, Mr Heep?
David *No!*
Traddles — and this is the end of my prosing on about myself. I don't make
  much, but I don't spend much ——
David — the recollection of Uriah sat heavy on me like a nightmare ——
Traddles — I board with the people downstairs, who are very agreeable
  people indeed ——
David The events of the night overtook me, my head was spinning again.
Agnes Mr and Mrs Heep.
Traddles Allow me to introduce them. This is Mr and Mrs Micawber.
David No! No!

SCENE 11

ADVERTISING!

Heep, Wickfield and Agnes withdraw

David, far from well, is staring up at Micawber and Mrs Micawber

Micawber Yes indeed *yes!* — Good heavens, Mr Traddles! To think that I
  should find you acquainted with the friend of my youth, the companion of
  earlier days!

David I fear I am not very well ...

Mrs Micawber Why, Mr Copperfield!

Micawber Will you take a drink, Mr Copperfield?

David (*very pale*) No!

Micawber Good! Here you are. I will drink to the days when my friend
Copperfield and I were younger, and when — in words we have sung
together before now — "We twa hae run about the braes, And pu'd the
gowans fine". I am not exactly aware what gowans may be, but I have no
doubt that Copperfield and myself would frequently have taken a pull at
them, if it had been feasible!

Mrs Micawber Mr Copperfield — I should like to have your opinion on Mr
Micawber's prospects. He is presently engaged in the sale of corn upon
commission, *but* — though corn may be gentlemanly, it is not remunerative. Commission to the extent of two and ninepence in a fortnight cannot,
however limited our ideas, be considered remunerative.

David } (*together*) No, not at all.
Traddles

Mrs Micawber I look around the world and say, "What is there in which a
person of Mr Micawber's talent is likely to succeed?"

David } (*together*) Of course.
Traddles

Mrs Micawber I have long felt the brewing business to be particularly
adapted to Mr Micawber, and the profits — I am told — are e-*nor*-mous.
But Mr Micawber cannot get into these firms — which decline to answer
his letters!

David } (*together*) Shocking!
Traddles

Mrs Micawber What is the conclusion, my dear Mr Copperfield, to which
I am irresistibly brought?

David Please ...

Traddles Tell us at once...

Mrs Micawber Things *cannot* be expected to turn up of themselves. We
must, in a measure, assist to turn them up.

David } (*together*) How!
Traddles

Mr Micawber } (*together*) By advertising!
Mrs Micawber

Mr Micawber In all the papers ——

Mrs Micawber — to describe himself plainly as so and so ——

Mr Micawber — with such and such qualifications ——

Mrs Micawber — and to put it thus ——

Mr Micawber "Now employ me, on remunerative terms, and address, post-
paid, to W.M., Post Office, Camden Town"!

SCENE 12

PARTING

The Lights go down on the Micawbers and Traddles

Dora appears

David My dearest darling! You have returned! My cup of happiness is full!
Dora Oh Doady — Sunday morning! It's the brightest time of the whole day,
  don't you think?
David It is bright now, though it was quite dark just a minute ago ...
Dora Do you mean a compliment — or has the weather really changed?
David It will be my birthday soon! And then your aunts will let us name the
  day!
Dora Will they be uncertain of which day it is?

Dora runs off

The Lights come up on Mr Peggotty on another part of the stage

Mr Peggotty My dear Davy: Not the best of news I fear. Mr Barkis more ill
  than ever, so Mr Chillip has little hope for him. It is a sad thing to see him
  so far gone. Always a good man though a little nearer than before. Will not
  part with half a crown for his own good. He does not complain, and, when
  he knows Clara, is as good a friend as she could wish for. God will take care
  of him I know.

*The Lights cross-fade to Steerforth and David. Rosa is at a distance, gently
  singing "The Curragh of Kildare"*

Peggotty goes

Steerforth So. It's all over with poor Barkis.
David I think I will go down and see my old nurse. It is no great effort to make
  for such a friend as she has been to me.
Steerforth (*restless, fervent*) It's a bad job — but the sun sets every day and
  people die every minute, and we mustn't be scared by the common lot. If
  we failed to hold our own, because that equal foot at all men's doors was
  heard knocking somewhere, every object in this world would slip from us.
  No! Ride on! Rough shod if need be, smooth shod if that will do, but ride
  on! Ride over all obstacles and win the race!
David And win what race?

Steerforth The race that one has started in. Ride on!
David I think I will ride down to see her.
Steerforth Well, go. You will do no harm.

Mrs Steerforth appears at a distance

Mrs Steerforth James!

Rosa stops singing

You are never here. Come and beg for my forgiveness.

Steerforth goes to Mrs Steerforth

Rosa (*watching Steerforth*) What is he doing?
David I don't understand you.
Rosa What is he doing? If you are honourable and faithful, I don't ask you
   to betray your friend. I ask you only to tell me, is it anger, is it hatred, is it
   pride, is it restlessness, is it some wild fancy, is it love, *what is it,* that is
   leading him?
David I know of nothing different in him. Nothing. I hardly understand what
   you mean.
Mrs Steerforth (*to Steerforth*) I understand you very well ——
Rosa Well there. I swear you to secrecy about this!
Mrs Steerforth — and cannot be angry with you long.

And Mrs Steerforth goes

After a moment, Steerforth approaches Rosa

Steerforth Come, Rosa, for the future we will love each other very much!
Rosa (*a sudden scream of rage, striking him*) Away! Get away from me! *Get
   away!*

Rosa runs out

David Steerforth, what is it that offends her?
Steerforth Anything you like, or nothing. She took everything, herself
   included, to a grindstone, and sharpened it. She is always dangerous.
   Good-night!
David Good-night! I shall be gone before you wake in the morning. Good-
   ' night!
Steerforth Daisy — if anything should ever separate us, you must think of
   me at my best, old boy.

David You have no best to me, Steerforth, and no worst. You are always equally loved and cherished in my heart.

Steerforth God bless you, Daisy. And good-night.

Steerforth climbs to a room and lies down

The Lights cross-fade to a light on Steerforth asleep and to another on David now with Young David

Music

David I was up with the dull dawn, and having dressed — looked into his room. He was fast asleep; lying easily, with his head upon his arm ——

Young David — as I had often seen him sleep at school.

David The time came soon when I almost wondered that nothing troubled his repose, but he slept ——

Young David — as I had often seen him sleep at school.

David And thus, in this silent hour, I left him.

SCENE 13

A DOUBLE LOSS

Barkis's room

Peggotty is at the bedside, and Mr Peggotty. Young David watches. Only Barkis can see Young David

The music fades

Peggotty Barkis, my dear! Here's my dear boy — here's Master Davy who brought us together, Barkis! That you sent messages by, you know! Won't you speak to Master Davy?

Mr Peggotty He's a goin' out with the tide.

David With the tide?

Mr Peggotty People can't die along the coast, except when the tide's pretty nigh out. They can't be born, unless it's pretty nigh in — not properly born, till flood. He's a goin' out with the tide …

Barkis (*very indistinct*) I shall — take you — to the stage — and they'll take you …

Young David Will you have a cake, Mr Barkis?

Barkis She make 'em?

Young David She makes all our pastry and does all our cooking.
Peggotty He's coming to himself. Barkis, my dear!
Barkis (*rising up a little*) Clara Peggotty Barkis — no better woman anywhere!
Peggotty (*indicating the older David*) Look! Here's Master Davy!
Barkis (*looking past him at Young David*) Barkis is willin'!

And Barkis rises and goes out with Young David

The rest bow their heads round the bed, and Peggotty bursts into tears

The music rises

David And it being low water, he went out with the tide …

The gentle mood of melancholy is broken by a great cry, a terrible, grief-stricken howl from Ham

Ham is amongst them

Ham Gone! Gone! Oh Mas'r Davy, Uncle!
David Ham, what's the matter?
Ham My love, Mas'r Davy — the pride and hope of my 'art — her that I'd have died for, and would die for now — she's gone!
Mr Peggotty (*dazed*) Tell me slow and careful. Tell me. Thank'ee, thank'ee, Ham my boy. Who's gone?
Ham Em'ly. Run away. But *how* she's run away. I pray God to kill her, rather than let her come to ruin and disgrace!
Mr Peggotty (*cry of rage*) What! *What?*
Ham (*giving it to David*) She left a letter ——
Mr Peggotty The man. I want to know his name — I want to know his name — his name.
Ham You doesn't ought to hear it.
Mr Peggotty I want to know his name.
Ham (*passionately*) His name is Steerforth! And he's a damned villain!

He pulls away a great black cloth or hanging which shows blood red inside, and reveals Steerforth and the aftermath of a bed scene

Emily stares out, frightened and bewildered

Emily (*pale, confused*) When I leave my home — it will be never to come back — unless he brings me back a lady … How my heart is torn … if you that I have wronged — could know what I suffer … Tell Uncle that I never loved him half so dear as now... Don't remember how affectionate and kind you've been to me ... Don't remember we were ever to be married — try to think as if I died when I was little, and was buried somewhere ... I'll pray for all — my last tears, and my last thanks, for Uncle!

And she runs back to Steerforth. A moment between them. They fade into darkness

Mr Peggotty snatches up his coat

Mr Peggotty I'm a going to seek my niece. I'm a going to seek my Em'ly. I'm a going first to stave in that theer boat, and sink it where I would have drownded him if I had had one thought of what was in him. As he sat afore me, face to face, strike me down dead, but I'd have drownded him, and thought it right! I tell you I'm a going to seek my niece!

Peggotty No, no, Dan'l, not as you are now! Seek her in a little while, and that'll be but right; but not as you are now. Let us speak a word about when she were young, and Ham was too. It'll soften your poor heart.

Mr Peggotty (*calmer*) I'll go tomorrow. I'm a going to seek her. That's my dooty evermore. (*To Peggotty*) You'll keep the old boat as it is. If ever she should come a wandering back, she might take heart to creep in, trembling; and might come to be laid down in her old bed, and rest her weary head where it was once so gay. (*A beat*) Do you go to London tomorrow, Mas'r Davy?

David Yes.

Mr Peggotty I'll go along with you — visit that man's mother ...

Peggotty takes him upstage, helps him into his coat, gives him his hat and case. David turns to Ham

David Ham? Ham? What are you thinking?

Ham On what's afore me, Mas'r Davy; and over yon ...

David On the life before you, do you mean?

Ham Ay, Mas'r Davy. I doen't rightly know how 'tis, but from over yon there seemed to me to come — the end of it like.

David What end?

Ham (*going*) I doen't know. I'm kinder muddled. Don't be afeer'd of me.

Ham goes

David shudders, unsteady on his feet

Young David appears

David turns, sees Young David, reaches out to him but can't get near

Young David (*plaintively*) Oh he's handsome. And bold. Brave as a lion. And you can't think how frank he is …

David Yes, yes I have never loved him better than now when the ties between us are broken … Even now … I could not reproach him … I hold in so much tenderness the memory of my affection for him.

Both Davids Handsome, and bold. Brave as a lion.

David But all is at an end between us!

Young David No!

David A cherished friend — *now dead*!

Young David *No!*

SCENE 14

SHE IS FAR BELOW HIM

Young David runs away in tears

David cannot follow him

Mrs Steerforth and Rosa appear. Mr Peggotty comes forward with his case and puts it down

Mr Peggotty I shouldn't feel it nat'ral to sit down in this house. I'd sooner stand.

Mrs Steerforth What do you want of me?

Mr Peggotty You've read my niece's letter. "Unless he brings me back a lady". I come to know, ma'am, whether he will keep his word.

Mrs Steerforth No.

Mr Peggotty Why not?

Mrs Steerforth It is impossible. He would disgrace himself. You cannot fail to know that she is far below him.

Mr Peggotty Raise her up!

Mrs Steerforth She is uneducated and ignorant.

Mr Peggotty Teach her better.

Mrs Steerforth Impossible!

Mr Peggotty You know what it is to love your child. So do I. If she were a hundred times my child I couldn't love her more. You don't know what it is to lose your child. I do. But, save her from this disgrace, and she shall never be disgraced by us. Not one of us that she's growed up among will ever look upon her pretty face again.

Mrs Steerforth I am sorry to repeat, it cannot be. If there is any other compensation ——

Mr Peggotty (*suddenly angry*) If your face don't turn to burning fire at the thought of offering money to me for my child's blight and ruin ——

Mrs Steerforth What compensation can you make to *me* for opening such a pit between me and my son? Let him put away his whim now, and he is welcome back. Let him *not* — and he never shall come near me, living or dying, unless — being rid of her forever — he comes to beg for my forgiveness. This is my right. This is the separation between us! And is this no injury?

Mrs Steerforth sweeps out

Rosa Why do you bring this man here?

David He is deeply injured. You may not know it ...

Rosa I know that James Steerforth has a false, corrupt heart, and is a traitor. But what need I know or care about this fellow and his common niece?

David You do him a great wrong!

Rosa They are worthless. I would have her whipped!

Mr Peggotty "passes on — without a word"

David For shame ——

Rosa I would trample on them all. I would have his house pulled down. I would have her branded on the face, dressed in rags, and cast out in the streets to starve. If there was any word of comfort that would be a solace to her in her dying hour, and only I possessed it, I wouldn't part with it for life itself.

SCENE 15

RUIN AND DISASTER!

Bailiffs cross the stage with furniture and bags. The Micawbers are in pursuit, followed by Traddles

Rosa and David melt away

Micawber Crushed!

Mrs Micawber Ruined!

Traddles A bit of a pull!

Bailiff We'll be back for the rug!

The Bailiff goes. Heep is suddenly amongst them

Heep Mr Micawber!
Micawber My dear Mr Heep, you find us at the very point of —
Heep (*cutting through*) Brokers?
Micawber Brokers.
Traddles From Tottenham Court Road.
Micawber In a state closely bordering on intoxication.
Heep May I beg to know?
Mrs Micawber Rent!
Micawber They have seized chattels and effects of every description.
Traddles And mine as well.
Micawber Dust and ashes, dust and ashes!

Another Bailiff goes by with a rug

No! Not the tasselled persian! *No!*
Heep (*to the Bailiffs*) Stop there! (*To Micawber*) You advertised.
Micawber I did.
Heep I saw you had.
Micawber I hoped you would —
Heep It's possible that I can, in a modest way, help you, Mr Micawber—
    provided always — you help me. I may need a clerk. A confidential clerk.
Micawber (*quickly*) I have already some acquaintance with the law.
Heep Oh?
Micawber As a defendant on a charge of bankruptcy.
Heep Of course.
Mrs Micawber I have always maintained that Mr Micawber possesses what
    I have heard my papa call — the judicial mind.
Heep It's not a persian rug at all. (*To the Bailiff*) Take it away.
Micawber Not persian? Observe the warp! Inspect the weft!
Mrs Micawber (*preoccupied*) But in applying himself to this subordinate
    branch of the law, can we be certain that he does not place it out of his power
    to rise — ultimately — to the top of the tree. As judge. Or even Chancellor?
    Would he be eligible?
Traddles (*cautiously*) He would be eligible.
Mrs Micawber My mind is at rest!
Micawber If I am reserved to wear a wig, my dear, I am at least prepared
    externally for that distinction!

Aunt Betsey, Mr Dick and David are in David's rooms

The Lights cross-fade to David's rooms

Traddles goes

Aunt Betsey Ruined!
Mr Dick Yes — she's ruined!
Aunt Betsey Yes — your aunt is ruined, Trot!
David I don't believe it!
Aunt Betsey I am ruined, my dear.
Mr Dick She told me before. She is ruined.
Aunt Betsey All I have in the world is in this room, except the cottage ——
Mr Dick She asked me if I were the philosopher she took me for, and I said yes I hope so, and she then said "I am ruined".
Aunt Betsey Ruined.
Mr Dick Splendid.
David But Mr Dick, ruin is no blessing — it leads to distress, want, starvation.
Mr Dick (*instantly in tears*) No, no! What can we do?
Aunt Betsey We must meet reverses boldly, and not suffer them to frighten us, my dear. We must learn to act the play out. We must live misfortune down, Dick!
David Aunt — for heaven's sake — tell me what has happened!
Aunt Betsey Something rum at Wickfield's. But that's between you and me, Trot.
David But, my dear Aunt — what can you mean?
Aunt Betsey He was a fine man of business — made a pretty penny for me — I don't deny it. But then he grew a little rusty …
David But surely Mr Wickfield would always use his best endeavours to secure your property.
Aunt Betsey His best endeavours. Yes. (*A beat*) The money's gone, Trot, there's no getting away from it. How shall we manage now? What will Dora say? What will her Aunts?

David, alarmed, hurries forward and starts to read a letter

Aunt Betsey and Mr Dick go

David To Wilkins Micawber, of Wickfield and Heep, Canterbury: With reference to my dear aunt's investments ——

The Lights cross-fade quickly to Micawber

During the following, Agnes joins David

Micawber To Mr David Copperfield, Buckingham Street, The Adelphi: I am here at my friend Heep's behest, in a capacity of confidence. I am here in a position of trust! The discussion of some topics, even with Mrs Micawber herself, is incompatible with the functions now devolving upon me. If I knew anything of the matter that you mention in your letter — I would sooner — like Oedipus — pluck out my tongue, than discuss affairs imparted — how shall I say — into my private ear ...

The Lights cross-fade quickly to David and Agnes

David Try not to be distressed. I am sure my aunt does not blame your father for her losses.
Agnes That is what she is good enough to tell me. Oh dear Trot — there is such a change at home. Uriah lives with us. The chief evil of his presence is that I cannot be as near Papa as I could wish, and cannot watch over him.
David And now they are partners, confound him!
Agnes If any fraud or treachery is practising against my father, I hope that simple love and truth will be stronger in the end.

The Lights cross-fade quickly to Mrs Micawber

Mrs Micawber To Mr David Copperfield, Buckingham Terrace, The Adelphi: Mr Micawber is entirely changed! He is reserved. He is secret. His life is a mystery to the partner of his joys and sorrows. But this is not all. He is morose, he is severe. You can form no adequate idea of his wildness, of his violence! Last night, on being childishly solicited for twopence, to buy lemon-stunners — a local sweetmeat — he drew an oyster-knife on the twins!

SCENE 16

NEWS!

A pool of light on Mr Peggotty praying

Mr Peggotty Dear Lord, only let her see my face — only let her hear my voice — only let my stanning still afore her bring to her thoughts the home she has fled away from. I've travelled far and wide to seek her, dreamt in my sleep that I raised her up and whispered to her: "Em'ly my dear, I am come fur to bring forgiveness, and to take you home!" Help me to find her I beg and pray, help me to bring her home.

The Lights cross-fade quickly to Rosa and David in Highgate

Rosa Has this girl been found?

David No.

Rosa And yet she has run away! She has run away from him. If she is not found, perhaps she will never be found. She may be dead.

David I am glad that time has softened you so much, Miss Dartle.

Rosa We have word from a servant of his. They went — they went to many countries. He took her to France, to Italy. He was quite attached to her. It seems incredible. She was admired — yes — he swears she was admired. Learnt to speak the languages. Never would have known her for a country girl. (*A beat*) And yet she was unhappy. Incredible. (*A beat*) But then he left her. Of course — he left her. Left her with this servant. Thought she could marry him. Thought she could marry him … (*A long, bitter laugh*) He did the honourable thing don't you think?

David What happened?

Rosa She went quite mad — had to be held by force — tried to get a knife — tried to get to the sea — tried to *beat her head* against the marble floor. One night she ran away. (*A beat*) She may be alive — for I believe some common things are hard to die. The servant thinks that he can find her — bring her to London. Show her to me.

A shaft of cold dawn light comes up on Mr Peggotty

Mr Peggotty I have knowed — awake or sleeping, as it was so true that I should find her — I have been so led on by it and held up by it — that I don't believe I can have been deceived. No! Em'ly's alive!

A light comes up on Emily, a tiny bedraggled figure, on another part of the stage

Emily He left me, but in my heart I'd left him before that — climbed down from the window — away from the man he left me with — ran away into the night — all the stars were shining — nobody must see me — blood on my feet, fire in my eyes, a great noise roaring in my head …

Rosa (*to David*) I'll send you word. The instant that I know her whereabouts.

Emily When I hear the wind blowing at night, I feel as if it was passing from him whose wife I should have been, and going up to God against me. I will pray for him with my last breath. Ham — whose wife I should have been …

A light reveals Ham, staring blankly out

Mr Peggotty (*in a whisper*) Ham — whose wife she should have been. He ain't no care — kinder no care no-how for his life. When there's any hard duty to be done with danger in it — he steps forward afore the rest …

*They are almost talking to one another. The wind blows louder, and the
Lights fade to Black-out*

SCENE 17

MARRIAGE!

Wedding music

*Dora, Aunt Betsey, Mr Dick, Peggotty, Agnes, Traddles and a Clergyman
hurry on. Their comments are an excited babble*

All (*ad lib*) The licence — have you forgotten? /Furniture to look at!/ A
kitchen fender and a meat screen!/ The dressmakers are here!/ Oh if you
please, Miss Dora, would you step upstairs?/ Agnes arrives at seven on the
coach./ Do you think it pretty, Doady?/ The ring — we must all see the
ring!/ Such a beautiful little house!/ How happy you will be here./ God
bless you, Trot!

David But I am happy — happy — in a dream, a flustered, happy, hurried
dream ... A misty and unsettled state, as if I had got up very early in the
morning a week or two ago, and had never been to bed since.

Traddles My congratulations!

David I hope the next time you come here, my dear fellow, it will be on the
same errand for yourself.

Traddles Thank you for your good wishes, my dear Copperfield. I assure
you, my dear boy, I am almost as pleased as if I were going to be married
myself!

David The rest is all a more or less incoherent dream ...

The wedding music is strong now

Vicar Of clergyman and clerk!

Agnes Of Agnes taking care of Dora ...

Aunt Betsey Of Betsy Trotwood endeavouring to represent herself as a
model of sternness ...

Dora Of Dora trembling very much and making her responses in faint
whispers ...

Mr Dick Of the signing of the register ...

Peggotty Of Peggotty going in to sign it ...

David Of walking proudly down the aisle with my sweet wife ...

Various (*ad lib*) Of whispering. / And laughing. / Of breakfast. / Of eating
and drinking. / Of speeches and tears and flowers. / Of the horses and the
carriage. / Of Dora being ready.

Dora (*weeping*) If I have ever been cross or ungrateful to anybody, don't remember it!

David My dear, dear wife …

Dora Are you happy now, you foolish boy? And sure you don't repent?

The guests stand stock still, the wedding veil lifts off; a clock ticks; David and Dora settle into chairs. A mess of presents and furniture around them

SCENE 18

MARRIED BLISS

David The honeymoon being over — I would think how queer it was that there we were, alone together — all the romance of our engagement put away upon a shelf, to rust.

All the guests, apart from Aunt Betsey and Traddles, melt away

One of our first feats in the housekeeping way was a little dinner to Traddles and Aunt Betsey.

Traddles and Aunt Betsey sit at the table. An awkward moment

David (*after a beat, to Dora*) My dearest life — do you think Mary Anne has any idea of time?

Dora Who?

David Our servant. You see, my love, it's five and we were to have dined at four.

Dora Oh. Perhaps the clock is fast.

David It's actually a few minutes slow.

Dora Naughty clock.

David Don't you think it would be better for you to remonstrate with Mary Anne?

Dora Oh no, please! I couldn't, Doady!

David But my love!

Dora No, no! Please! Don't be a naughty bluebeard! Don't be serious!

David My love — how you tremble!

Dora Because I *know* you're going to scold me.

David My sweet, I am only going to reason.

Dora Oh but reasoning is worse than scolding! I didn't marry to be reasoned with. You must be sorry that you married me, or else you wouldn't reason with me.

A slatternly servant — clearly drunk — staggers in with two covered dishes, bangs them down on the table and goes

David My love — what have you got in that dish?
Dora Mutton.
Traddles (*observing the joint*) What an extraordinary shape!
David I often wonder whether our butcher contracts for all the deformed sheep that come into the world … (*Cutting into it*) Raw!
Traddles (*helpfully*) Just how I like it!
David Yesterday dinner arrived as I was leaving the house, the day before I was made quite unwell by being obliged to eat raw veal in a hurry — this is not comfortable!
Dora (*suddenly in tears*) Oh you cruel, cruel boy, to say I am a disagreeable wife!
David My dear Dora — I never said that!
Dora You said I wasn't comfortable!
David The housekeeping is not comfortable…
Dora (*rushing out in tears*) It's exactly the same thing!

Dora goes

Another awkward moment

Traddles It looks delicious.

Traddles goes in pursuit

Aunt Betsey You must have patience, Trot.

SCENE 19

Micawber — Fraud Squad!

The Lights come up quickly on Micawber

During the following there is the rumble of carriage wheels and the wild neighing of horses

Micawber My dear Copperfield: Without more directly referring to any latent ability that may possibly exist on my part, of wielding the thunderbolt, or directing the devouring and avenging flame in any quarter, I may be permitted to observe, in passing, that my brightest visions are forever dispelled — that my peace is shattered and my power of enjoyment destroyed. You will ask, you will demand, you will insist: What is the matter? Villainy is the matter; baseness is the matter; deception, fraud and conspiracy are the matter! But I will not digress. Direct your footsteps with haste to the Canterbury coach, fly with it southwards, seek out the house of Wickfield — I shall be there to meet you.

David emerges from the darkness

David I arrived the next evening — sensing that even when due allowance had been made for Mr Micawber's lofty style of composition, something important lay at the bottom of it.
Micawber (*coming forward*) My dear Copperfield.

Heep appears suddenly

Heep What an unexpected and delightful pleasure — if I may be allowed to say so. Micawber! Return to the office, if you please.
David After dinner that night, Agnes retired, and Uriah coaxed her father into glass on glass of wine.

The Lights come up on Wickfield in his room

Heep and David join him. Micawber looks on

Wickfield (*unsteadily*) I drink to your charming and delightful aunt. I drink to her patient understanding.
Heep (*excitedly*) And I'll give you another! And I 'umbly ask for bumpers, seeing I intend to make it the divinest of her sex.
Wickfield (*weakly*) No …
Heep (*not hearing*) I'm a humble individual to give you her 'elth, but I admire — adore her!
Wickfield (*barely audible*) No — please …
Heep Agnes Wickfield is the divinest of her sex. May I speak out amongst friends? To be her father is a proud distinction, but to be her 'usband ——
Wickfield (*a great cry*) No! No!
Heep What's the matter? You are not gone mad I hope? I've an ambition to make your Agnes my Agnes. I have as good a right as another man.
Wickfield (*beside himself*) Look at him, look at him!
David Calm yourself, I beg you, this will do no good ——
Wickfield Only look at him!
David Think of Agnes, think of her hearing you or seeing you like this; spare her the agony of such a scene!
Wickfield Look at my torturer. Before him I have step by step abandoned name and reputation, peace and quiet, house and home!

Heep You had better stop him, Copperfield, if you can. He'll say something presently he'll be sorry to have said afterwards ——

Wickfield (*passionate*) I'll say anything! Why should I not be in the world's power if I am in yours!

Heep Because you have a daughter! You and me know what we know, don't we? Let sleeping dogs lie — who wants to rouse 'em?

Wickfield (*suddenly tired*) Weak indulgence has ruined me. Oh Trotwood, I don't know all I have done in my fatuity. *He* knows best — for he has always been at my elbow — whispering me. You find him in my house, you find him in my business. You heard him but a little time ago. What need have I to say more?

And Wickfield goes unsteadily from the room

Heep I didn't expect he'd cut up so rough, Master Copperfield, but it's nothing—I'll be friends with him tomorrow. When a person's 'umble, you know, what's an apology? So easy! (*A beat*) I suppose you have sometimes plucked a pear before it was ripe?

David I suppose I have.

Heep I've just done that — but it'll ripen yet! It only wants attending to. I can wait.

Heep goes

Micawber grabs David

Micawber There is more — so much more; you have not grasped a hundred thousandth of the villainy!

David What's to be done?

Micawber The struggle is over! I will lead this life no longer. I am a wretched being, cut off from everything that makes life tolerable. I am a straw upon the surface of the deep, and am tossed in all directions by the elephants — I beg your pardon; I should have said — the elements!

David Calm yourself, steady yourself!

Micawber (*beside himself*) Not till I have — blown to fragments — the — a — detestable serpent — Heep. I'll partake of no man's hospitality, until I have — a — moved Mount Vesuvius — to eruption — on — a — the abandoned rascal — *Heep*! This day week — a — at breakfast time — everybody must be present including Mr Traddles — plus — a — Aunt — a — and friendly gentleman with kite — to be here where myself — a — will expose intolerable ruffian — *Heep*! No more to say — a — or listen to persuasion — go immediately — not capable — a — bear society — upon the track of devoted and doomed traitor — *Heep*!

Scene 20

Denunciation

A dim light comes up on another part of the stage

Rosa Dartle confronts Emily

Rosa I have come to see James Steerforth's fancy, the girl who is the town
talk of her native place...
Emily Who are you?
Rosa One who used to know him.
Emily How have you found me?
Rosa His servant told me.
Emily Let me go.
Rosa Stay there — or I'll proclaim you to the house, to the whole street!
Emily Spare me — if you would be spared yourself!
Rosa I wonder if you know what you have done. Do you ever think of the
home you have laid waste?
Emily Is there ever night or day when I don't think of it! My lost home ...
Rosa *Your* home! I speak of *his* home — where I live. Look at you! A worthy
cause of division between mother and son — a piece of pollution, picked
up from the waterside, to be made much of for an hour, and then tossed back
to her original place!
Emily No! I had been brought up as virtuous as you or any lady. If you live
in his home and know him, you know what his power might be. He used
all his power to deceive me, and I believed him, trusted him, and loved him!

Rosa strikes at her in a passion. Real malignity

Rosa You love him? You? They should whip creatures like you! (*A beat.
Calmer*) If I could order it to be done, I would have you whipped to death.
I am of a strange nature perhaps, but I can't breathe freely in the air you
breathe. I find it sickly. Therefore I will have it cleared; I will have it
purified of you. If you live here tomorrow, I'll have your story and your
character proclaimed on the common stair, on the street, in any place where
you pretend to any character but your true one. Or die! There are doorways
and dust-heaps for such deaths — find one, and take your flight to Heaven!
Mr Peggotty (*off*) Em'ly! My darling girl! My Em'ly!
Rosa Mark me. What I say — I mean to do.

Mr Peggotty bursts in

Mr Peggotty Em'ly! Em'ly — my love!

Emily Uncle! Oh Uncle!

Mr Peggotty (*gathering her in his arms*) My dream's come true! My
dream's come true! I thank God for it, I thank God for having guided me
to my darling. Oh Em'ly, Em'ly. (*Picking her up*) Come away now. Now
you're found, you're found. I never have stopped loving you. Never, never,
never …

Scene 21

The Child-Wife

Mr Peggotty carries her away

The room fades from sight

*Dora appears from the new home and takes David's coat, then turns to her
household accounts. Young David watches her*

David It was now some months since our marriage. Our domestic life grew
no easier. Everybody seemed to cheat us. Our appearance in a shop was a
signal for the damaged goods to be brought out immediately. We might
have kept the basement storey paved with butter — such was our apparent
consumption of it. And as to the washerwoman pawning the clothes, well
— I suppose that might have happened several times to anybody …

Dora These numbers — they won't come right. They make my head ache
so. And they won't do anything I want …

David Let us try together, Dora. Now — do not cry or be ridiculous. You
must learn a little firmness!

Young David No!

David Only to form her mind.

Young David Why do you bother her. Leave her alone. Murderer!

David I could have wished my wife had been my counsellor ——

Young David She is pretty and young and you must leave her alone!

David I love her dearly, and I am happy — but the happiness I had anticipated
is not the happiness I feel now … there is something wanting …

Young David What do you miss?

David Something that was a dream of yours …

Young David Yes! (*Prompting him*) And they all lived happy and content
for ever after.

Dora Will you call me your child-wife?

David (*laughing*) Why?

Dora When you are going to be angry with me, say to yourself "it's only my
child-wife". When you miss what I should like to be, and think can never
be, say "still my foolish child-wife loves me".

Young David Why should you seek to change what has been so precious to you for so long? She never can be better than her own natural self. No more firmness! No more forming her mind!

David I always loved her. But as the year had passed Dora was not strong.

Sad music. Dora goes to lie on the bed

I had hoped that a baby on her breast might change my child-wife to a woman. But it was not to be. The spirit fluttered for a moment on the threshold of its little prison, and unconscious of captivity, took wing.

Young David (*urgently riffling through David's papers*) No — Don't let her die …

David When I carried her upstairs every night and felt she was lighter in my arms, a dead blank feeling came upon me, as if I were approaching to some dead frozen region yet unseen that numbed my life.

Young David How do you think of her?

David As she was before.

Young David How do you remember her?

David No! Not yet. I cannot leave her.

Mr Peggotty appears

Mr Peggotty Em'ly put these flowers by for Mrs Copperfield. I hope they find her well!

Dora When I can run about again as I used to, I shall gather twice this bunch for her.

David How is Emily?

Mr Peggotty 'Tis little as she has said in wureds, but we knows full well as we can put our trust in one another ever more.

David And the future?

Mr Peggotty Theer's mighty countries far from here. Our future lies over the sea. 'Twas hard to say farewell back home. My good sister'll take care of Ham — poor fellow. Em'ly's written to him, sir. I thought perhaps ——

David I'll take the letter to him. Of course I will.

Mr Peggotty God bless you, sir. God bless you.

Mr Peggotty turns and goes

David The time Mr Micawber had appointed so mysteriously at last arrived. My aunt and I were unwilling to leave Dora.

Aunt Betsey, Traddles, and Mr Dick gather at Dora's bedside

Young David joins them

Dora I won't speak to you. I'll be disagreeable. I shall be sure you really are "a cross old thing" if you don't go!

David It could all be a whim of Micawber's. Nothing to it.

Traddles Micawber's been in touch with me, you know. I have to say that his — um — disclosure, is of a — a highly important nature.

Dora For Agnes, Doady.

Aunt Betsey You know you can't do without *me*!

Dora Yes I can! Now listen. You must all go. I am not very ill indeed. Am I?

Aunt Betsey Why, what a question!

David No ...

Dora You must go now, or I shall not believe you.

SCENE 22

MONSTER OF MEANNESS

Change of mood, change of light

Aunt Betsey, Mr Dick and Traddles move from Dora's bedside

Young David stays with her and they watch the next scene. It is Canterbury. Wickfield's office

David (*as though recounting the day's events to Dora*) So we four, that is to say, my aunt, Mr Dick, Traddles and I, went down to Canterbury by the Dover mail that very day!

Micawber (*sotto voce*) My dear friends! May I beg you to do me the favour to submit yourselves, for the moment to the direction of one who — though crushed out of his original form by individual errors — is still your fellow man.

David We have perfect confidence in you, and will do as you please!

Micawber (*gratefully*) My dear Copperfield — I hope I see you well?

David Is Mr Wickfield at home?

Micawber Mr Wickfield is unwell in bed, sir, of a rheumatic fever, but Miss Wickfield will be happy to see old friends.

Agnes arrives

Cries of delighted greeting between the old friends

Micawber flings open the office door

Miss Trotwood, Mr David Copperfield, Mr Thomas Traddles, and Mr Dick.

Heep (*starting up*) Well I am sure this is indeed an unexpected pleasure …
  Mr Copperfield — I hope I see you well. Mrs Copperfield, sir, I hope she's
  getting on. We have been made quite uneasy by the poor accounts we have
  had of her state, lately, I do assure you … Don't wait, Micawber. (*A beat*)
  What are you waiting for? Why do you wait?

Micawber Because I — in short — choose.

Heep I'm afraid you'll oblige me to get rid of you. Go along! I'll talk to you
  presently.

Micawber (*bursting out*) If there is a scoundrel on this earth with whom I
  have already talked too much, that scoundrel's name is — *Heep*!

Heep (*looking slowly round*) Oho! This is a conspiracy! You have met here,
  by appointment! You are playing booty with my clerk, are you, Copperfield? Now, take care. There's no love between us, I know. You were
  always a puppy with a proud stomach, and you envy me my rise, do you?
  Miss Wickfield, if you have any love for your father, you had better not join
  this gang. I'll ruin him if you do …

Traddles As for Miss Wickfield's father — I am his agent and friend, and
  have a power of attorney from him in my pocket.

Heep The old ass has drunk himself into a state of dotage, and it has been got
  from him by fraud!

Traddles Something has been got from him by fraud, I know. Now then —
  Mr Micawber ——

Micawber (*producing a large document*) Dear Miss Trotwood and gentlemen ——

Aunt Betsey Bless and save the man! He'd write letters by the ream, if it was
  a capital offence!

Micawber — In an accumulation of ignominy, want, despair, and madness,
  I entered the office — or as our lively neighbour the Gaul would term it,
  the bureau — of the Firm, nominally conducted under the name of
  Wickfield and Heep, but in reality, wielded by Heep alone. Heep, and Heep
  alone, is the forger and cheat.

Heep (*lunging at Micawber*) The devil take you!

Micawber (*side-stepping and belabouring Heep with his ruler*) Sit down,
  sir, or by heaven I'll split your skull! Sit down, you cur! (*Composing
  himself*) Heep rendered me so derisory a pittance by way of remuneration,
  that it soon became necessary for me to solicit from Heep — pecuniary
  advances towards the support of my family. Thus I became emmeshed in
  the web he had spun for my reception and found that — now in debt to Heep
  — my services were constantly called upon for the falsification of
  business, and the mystification of an individual whom I shall designate —
  Mr W. My charges against Heep are as follows: first, when Mr W's
  faculties and memory became weakened and confused, Heep induced him
  to draw out one very large sum of trust money to meet pretended business

charges. He gave this proceeding, throughout, the appearance of having originated in Mr W's own dishonest intention, and has used it ever since, to torture and constrain him!

Heep You shall prove this, you Copperfield! All in good time!

Micawber Ask — Heep — if he ever kept a pocket book in this house. Or ask him if he ever burnt one here. If he says yes, and asks you where the ashes are, refer him to Wilkins Micawber!

Heep (*another lunge at Micawber*) Damn you!

Micawber parries as before; much snapping and snarling from Heep and growling and barking from Micawber

Micawber (*resuming his letter*) My second charge against Heep is as follows: that the filial affection of Mr W's daughter was to be secretly influenced to prevent any investigation of the firm's affairs after her father's death.

Heep What more have you got to bring forward?

Micawber Third and last. I can show, that Heep has systematically forged the signature of Mr W and I can prove by Heep's false books, and Heep's real memoranda — as well as the incriminating charred remnants of his pocket book, that Mr W has for years been deluded and plundered in every conceivable manner, to the pecuniary aggrandisement of the avaricious, false, and grasping — Heep, whose most recent act was to persuade Mr W to relinquish his share in the partnership. Heep has the deed about him. And thus, ladies and gentlemen, have his meshes gradually thickened, until the unhappy Mr W could see no world beyond. Bankrupt as he believed, alike in circumstances, in all hope, and in honour — his sole reliance was upon this monster in the garb of man!

Mr Dick Bravo!

Micawber One moment if you please. (*He hasn't quite finished*) I have now concluded. It merely remains for me to substantiate these accusations; and then, with my ill-starred family, to disappear from the landscape on which we appear to be an encumbrance.

Protests from his allies

Let it be, in justice, merely said of me, as of a gallant and eminent naval hero, with whom I have no pretensions to cope, that what I have done, I did, in despite of mercenary and selfish objects — "For England, home and Beauty"!

Heep makes a sudden dash to open the drawer of a desk

Heep Where are the books? Some thief has stolen the books!

Traddles Don't be uneasy. They have come into my possession. I will take care of them, under the authority I mentioned.

Aunt Betsey (*making a dash at him*) You know what I want?

Heep A strait jacket ——

Aunt Betsey No. My property! Agnes, my dear, as long as I thought your father had lost it — I was content to keep my peace ——

Agnes Miss Trotwood ——

Aunt Betsey Agnes — not a word! *But*, now I know this fellow's answerable for it — and I'll have it!

Heep What do you want done?

Traddles First, the deed of relinquishment must be given over to me now — here. Then you must prepare to disgorge all that your rapacity has become possessed of

Heep Must? I don't know about that!

Traddles Maidstone Jail is a safe place of detention while you consider the situation. Copperfield, will you go round to the Guildhall and bring a couple of officers?

Heep (*frightened*) Stop! (*Very reluctantly*) Here's the deed . As for the rest—

Traddles It must be done without delay!

Heep (*cornered, snarling*) Copperfield, I have always hated you. You've always been an upstart, and you've always been against me!

David It is you who have been, in your greed and cunning against all the world. But greed and cunning over-reach themselves. It is as certain as death.

Heep Or as certain as they used to teach at school — from nine o'clock to eleven that labour was a curse; and from eleven o'clock to one, that it was a blessing and a cheerfulness and a dignity and I don't know what. You preach about as consistent as they did. Won't 'umbleness go down? I shouldn't have got round my gentleman fellow partner without it, I think. (*A beat*) *Micawber* — you old bully, I'll pay *you*!

A final clash between Micawber and Heep: thrusts and yelps and barking

Heep is chased from the house

An outburst of joy and celebration

Aunt Betsey A monster of meanness!

Traddles He is such an incarnate hypocrite, that whatever object he pursues, he must pursue crookedly.

Mrs Micawber appears at the door

Micawber Emma, Emma my love! Come in, come in! The cloud between
· us is past, the cloud is past!

Micawber gives Mrs Micawber an emotional hug

Now welcome poverty! Welcome misery, welcome houselessness, wel-
come hunger, rags, tempest and beggary ——
Aunt Betsey Mr Micawber—I wonder you have never turned your thoughts
to emigration.
Micawber The Antipodes?
Aunt Betsey Why yes!
Micawber Madam, it was the dream of my youth, and the fallacious
aspiration of my riper years.
Aunt Betsey What a thing it would be for your family — if you were to
emigrate now.
Micawber Capital, madam, capital.
Mrs Micawber That is the principal, I may say the only difficulty.
Aunt Betsey Capital? But you have done us a great service, and what could
we do for you, that would be half so good as to find the capital?
Micawber I could not receive it as a gift! (*A longish pause as his resolve
melts*) *But* if a sufficient sum could be advanced, say at five percent interest
per annum upon my personal liability.
Aunt Betsey Could be? Can be, and shall be, on your own terms!
Mrs Micawber There is but one question, my dear ma'am, I could wish to
ask. The climate I believe is healthy.
Aunt Betsey Finest in the world!
Mrs Micawber Just so. Then my question arises. Now, *are* the circumstances
of the country such, that a man of Mr Micawber's abilities would have a
fair chance of rising in the social scale? I will not say at present, might he
aspire to be Governor, or anything of that sort — but would there be a
reasonable opening for his talents to develop themselves?
Aunt Betsey No better opening anywhere!
Mrs Micawber Then I am quite, quite satisfied!
Micawber The feeling, my love, is entirely mutual.

SCENE 23

DARKNESS

*Micawber launches into a ballad: "List to the Convent Bells" (see notes on
page viii) Everybody joins in and, arm in arm, leaves the stage*

David is left with Dora and Young David

The Lights change

David All else grows dim and fades away. I am again with Dora in our cottage. I do not know how long she has been ill. I am so used to it in feeling that I cannot count the time. It is night. Agnes has arrived ...

Agnes is beside him

Music underscores

Dora I am afraid I was too young.
David No!
Dora I don't mean in years only, but in experience, and thoughts, and everything. I'm afraid it would have been better if we had only loved each other as a boy and girl, and forgotten it.
David We have been very happy.
Dora Yes, oh yes. But as the years went on, you would have wearied of your child-wife. She wouldn't have improved. It is better as it is.
David Dora, my dearest, dearest — do not speak to me so.
Dora How he cries. Hush, hush. Do one thing for me. I want to speak to Agnes — quite alone. Go downstairs and leave us for a while.

David moves away. Agnes leans close to her, nods as she whispers in her ear. Dora lies back. Young David takes Dora's hand and leads her down and away. As they pass David, Young David gives him a sheet of paper

Young David and Dora dance a single solemn step before they vanish

The music fades

David (*reading*) "It is over. Darkness comes before my eyes; and for a time, all things are blotted out of my remembrance. The future is walled up before me, there will be no refuge for me but in the grave. But I have one last commission to discharge. Emily's letter to Ham ... I must go down to Yarmouth ... take the coach ..."

SCENE 24

TEMPEST

The distant noise of a storm, as at the start of the play

David stands, slowly, facing front. He is adrift — under pressure, troubled, abstracted. The Company gather around him, dressed in capes and sou'westers; braced against the wind

Company 1 A terrible storm sir, the worst I can remember.

Ham is at David's side. He takes and looks at the letter

Ham I thank'ee, sir, most kind. I'm not like to see my uncle or Em'ly again. Beg her to forgive me.
David What for?
Ham For pressing my affections on her. If I hadn't — she might have told me what was struggling in her mind. I might have saved her. Tell her I still love her, mourn for her, but ease her mind and say that I'm not tired of this life. But say that no-one could ever be to me what she was.

The storm roars up again. In the midst of this — a verse of the storm song (see music notes on page viii). The Company shift ropes, are thrown about by the wind, cling to one another

Company   The tremendous sea falling
                     Batters the shore;
                     Old enemies brawling.
                     The loud waves roaring…

Wind, noise, waves crashing. A door slams

David at night in the Inn

The storm outside. Shutters groan and creak

David Depressed in spirits … solitary, uneasy, seriously affected — without knowing how much — by late events. Confused by the long exposure to this wind — this fierce wind …
Voices (*yelling against the wind*) Two gone down — with all hands ——
Voices Tea clipper workin' hard to keep off shore ——
Voices Two, three more in distress — labouring hard in the Roads …
David A jumble in my thoughts and recollections … quite lost the sense of time and distance … odd, odd — a curious inattention in my mind … but busy too … all the remembrances of the place — distinct and vivid. At night — new terrors, real and fanciful. And I can *see nothing* — only my own haggard face looking in at me from the black void!

Storm, fury. Second sea verse

Company   Mercy on poor sailors, dying
                     Shattered in the waves;
                     Hear the poor souls crying
                     In their boiling graves...

*Storm, fury. The cast gather, linked by a great rope. An agony of horror at
what they are witnessing just off shore. The winds buffet them*

David (*yelling*) What is it?!
Voice A wreck — way out yonder!
David What wreck?
Voice See! There! A schooner! From Spain or Portugal!
David Great Heaven! I see it!
Voice Mizen mast gone!
Voice Dear God help them!
Voice Get to it! Cut it free! For the love of God, cut the rigging free!
David Too late!
Voice They're lost — gone!
David No! One man left there, up on the second mast!
Voice She's parting amidships! She'll break up any moment!
Voices (*screaming*) Save him — mercy on us! — save him!
David Do something for him, God help him!

Ham breaks through the crowd

Ham I'll try my chance.
David No, no! I beg you! It's impossible — madness!
Ham Mas'r Davy — if my time is come, 'tis come. If 'tan't, I'll bide it. Lord
     above bless you, and bless all! Friends — hold firm! I'm a going out!

*The storm surges up again The men take the strain on the rope round Ham's
waist. He wades out into the sea (this could be up stage, and out into the
audience). Third sea verse*

Company   Striding, leaping, swimming, striving
                     Driving on; the lost ship breaking;
                     Hope reviving, waning, dimming
                     Tossed and ripped, the waters shake him!

*Sudden silence. We see Ham grapple with the figure (Steerforth) on a mast,
clinging to a rope. In silence they turn and turn about — back to the shore.
A sudden crash of thunder and sea din. Ham drops Steerforth, and is thrown
further up on the beach*

David Dead! He's dead! No … No …
Voice Carry him back, carry him back! Make way there!
Voice He's gone. The last wave did for him …
David Generous heart, generous, generous heart — stilled for ever.
Voice Sir, he brought a body back with him.
Voice Sir — look, look!
David Do I know it?
Voice Sir!

They take him to Steerforth's body

David (*appalled, aghast*) Steerforth … Steerforth…

The crowd melt away. Rosa Dartle stands behind David

Rosa (*ferocious*) I loved him better than she ever loved him! Proud mother
of a proud, false son! And is your pride appeased? *Now* he has made
atonement to you — with his life! He gave me this scar — but I would have
been his slave for a word of love a year. What is your love to mine?
David Forgive his faults ——
Rosa Faults! Who dares malign him? He had a soul worth millions of the
friends to whom he stooped!

The Lights go out on Rosa. The stage is still. Everybody is waiting

David So much sadness, the ghosts of so many hopes, of so many memories,
many errors, many unavailing sorrows and regrets. I have lost love,
friendship, interest, my first trust, my first affection, the whole airy castle
of my life.
Aunt Betsey No. Trotwood.

David doesn't hear her

Trotwood. Agnes … I think Agnes is going to be married.
David (*faintly*) God bless her …
Aunt Betsey God bless her — (*moving to David*) — and her husband too.

Agnes is standing at the back

Agnes David! (*After a moment*) David *Copperfield* …

The Company echo the name. Acknowledging him. David looks up at Agnes

David (*slowly*) David Copperfield…

The Lights fade to Black-out

CURTAIN

FURNITURE AND PROPERTY LIST

ACT I

Young David: lamp (practical)
Desk. *On it*: papers, etc.
Desk chair
Aunt Betsey: ear muffs, bags

Table. *On it*: plates, spoons
5 chairs

Chairs
Desk. *On it*: books, papers, pencil
Murdstone: cane

Boxes, bags (on containing cakes)
School trunk

Huge blackboard
Creakle: cane
Desk. *On it*: papers, books, etc.
Placard: "TAKE CARE OF HIM HE BITES"
Chairs

Coffin. *On it*: funeral pall with flower petals one side, travelling rug on reverse side
Baskets
Bags

Crates of bottle
Washing tub
Desk

Mrs Micawber: various belongings, handkerchief
Micawber: handkerchief
Young David: bags, money

Shop counter

Mr Dick: 7 foot kite made out of closely-written manuscript
Chairs
Desk

ACT II

Chairs
Tables. *On them*: tablecloths

Travelling bags

Chairs
Table. *On it*: bottle of wine, 3 glasses
Traddles: 6 bottle of wine, coins

Couch
Coats

Bed

Black cloth, blood red on reverse
Mr Peggotty: coat
Peggoty's hat and case

Bailiffs: furniture, bags, rug

David: letter

Chairs
Table. *On it*: cutlery, plates, carving knife and fork
Wedding presents
Servant: 2 covered dishes

Wickfield: glass of wine

Desk. *On it*: papers, pen
Chairs
Bed

Desk. *On it*: ruler
Chairs
Micawber: large document
Young David: letter

Ropes
Large rope linking the **Company**
Mast

LIGHTING PLOT

Property fittings required: nil

Various interior and exterior settings

ACT I

To open: Dim light on **Young David**

Cue 1	**Young David**: "Where are you hid?" *Bring up lighting on* **David**	(Page 1)
Cue 2	**David**: " ...from the *black void* ..." *Snap on bright sunshine effect on Blunderstone area*	(Page 1)
Cue 3	**Peggotty**: "Now these Cronkindales ..." *Bring up lighting on* **Murdstone** *group*	(Page 5)
Cue 4	**Murdstone, Quinion** and **Passnidge** go *Fade lighting on* **Murdstone** *group; reduce lighting on Blunderstone area*	(Page 7)
Cue 5	To open SCENE 5 *Cross-fade to Yarmouth area; interior effect on boat house*	(Page 8)
Cue 6	**Mr Peggotty**: " ... such a thing again!" *Cross-fade to bright morning effect on beach area*	(Page 9)
Cue 7	**Emily**: "Look here!" *Intense follow spot on* **Emily**	(Page 10)
Cue 8	**Emily** laughs and runs back to **Young David** *Cut follow spot*	(Page 10)
Cue 9	**David**: " ... was piercing." *Lighting becomes chilly*	(Page 10)
Cue 10	**Young David** flings himself on his bed *Cross-fade to lighting on* **Young David** *and* **David**	(Page 12)

Cue 11	**Young David**: "... hate him."	(Page 12)
	Cross-fade to general lighting on best parlour area	
Cue 12	**Murdstone**: " ... will go upstairs, boy."	(page 13)
	*Bring up lighting on **David**'s bedroom area*	
Cue 13	The loud sound of the door being locked	(Page 14)
	*Lighting concentrates on **Young David***	
Cue 14	**Young David**: "... I sent 'em all my love."	(Page 15)
	Cross-fade to general lighting on best parlour area	
Cue 15	**David**: "So I lost her."	(Page 15)
	*Cross-fade to lighting on **Barkis** and **Young David***	
Cue 16	**Mr Mell**: "Down by Blackheath."	(Page 17)
	Cross-fade to lighting on school room	
Cue 17	**David**: "... *infinitely less mischief*!"	(Page 18)
	Reduce to night time effect on domitory area	
Cue 18	They bang on **Steerforth**'s door	(Page 19)
	*Bring up lighting on **Steerforth***	
Cue 19	**Steerforth**: "Good-night, young Copperfield."	(Page 21)
	Cross-fade to lighting on school room	
Cue 20	**Creakle** and **Tungay** turn and follow **Mr Mell**	(Page 23)
	Reduce to night time effect	
Cue 21	**David**: "... Steerforth came to me."	(Page 23)
	Increase to exterior daylight effect	
Cue 22	**Young David**: " ... and don't truly wish it!"	(Page 29)
	Reduce to night time effect	
Cue 23	**David**: " ... with a baby at her breast."	(Page 31)
	*Cross-fade to interior effect on the **Micawbers***	
Cue 24	**Micawber**: "We shall venture out."	(Page 33)
	Cross-fade to exterior effect	
Cue 25	**Micawber**: "Catastrophe!"	(Page 34)
	Cross-fade to dim lighting on prison area with window shadow effect	
Cue 26	**Young David**: "Yes."	(Page 36)
	Cross-fade to general lighting	

Cue 27	**Janet**: " ... and that's all I have got to say." *Cross-fade to* **Aunt Betsey**'s *house and garden*	(Page 40)
Cue 28	**Aunt Betsey, Young David** and **Mr Dick** go *Cross-fade to* **Wickfield**'s *study*	(Page 46)
Cue 29	**Company**: "To you, our hearts we pledge!" *Reduce lighting, bring up fireglow effect*	(Page 48)
Cue 30	**Young David** leaves **Wickfield** *Cross-fade to dim lighting on* **Young David** *alone*	(Page 48)
Cue 31	**Wickfield** approaches with **Dora** *Bring up general lighting*	(Page 49)
Cue 32	**David**, **Dora** and **Young David** dance *Fade to black-out*	(Page 50)

ACT II

To open: Snap up lighting on **David**

Cue 33	**Dora** goes *Cross-fade to general light on another area of the stage*	(Page 51)
Cue 34	**Steerforth** goes *Bring up light on* **Young David**	(Page 52)
Cue 35	**David**: "Young — young ..." *Reduce to lighting on* **Micawber** *and* **David**	(Page 53)
Cue 36	**David**: " ... to Highgate!" *Bring up general lighting on Highgate area*	(Page 54)
Cue 37	**Rosa**: "Well, that's quite delightful." *Lighting change to denote passage of time*	(Page 55)
Cue 38	The **Peggotty** group invade the scene *Change lighting to suggest Yarmouth, focusing on* **Peggoty** *group*	(Page 56)
Cue 39	The **Peggoty** family and **Emily** move to the boathouse *Revert to previous lighting*	(Page 56)
Cue 40	**Mrs Steerforth** and **Rosa** go *Cross-fade to the boathouse area*	(Page 57)

Cue 41	**Emily**: " ... changeable like me ..." *Cross-fade to light on* **Dora**	(Page 60)
Cue 42	**David**: " ... admiration of all concerned." *Cross-fade to Highgate area*	(Page 60)
Cue 43	**Steerforth**: " ... she was born to be a lady." *Cross-fade to* **Aunt Betsey**	(Page 60)
Cue 44	**Steerforth**, **Traddles** and **David** move off to the party *Cross-fade to party area*	(Page 64)
Cue 45	**Traddles**: " ... than I have." *Cross-fade to* **Agnes**, **Wickfield** and **Heep**	(Page 68)
Cue 46	**David**: "No! No!" *Cross-fade to the* **Micawbers**	(Page 68)
Cue 47	**Mr Micawber**: " '... Camden Town'!" *Cross-fade to* **Dora**	(Page 69)
Cue 48	**Dora** runs off *Cross-fade to* **Mr Peggotty**	(Page 70)
Cue 49	**Mr Peggoty**: "God will take care of him I know." *Cross-fade to* **Steerforth** and **David**	(Page 70)
Cue 50	**Steerforth** climbs to a room and lies down *Cross-fade to light on* **Steerforth** *and another on* **David** with **Young David**	(Page 72)
Cue 51	**David**: "... I left him." *Cross-fade to* **Barkis**'*s room*	(Page 72)
Cue 52	**Ham** pulls away a great black cloth *Bring up light on* **Steerforth**	(Page 73)
Cue 53	**Emily** runs back to **Steerforth**. A moment *Fade light light on* **Steerforth** *and* **Emily**	(Page 74)
Cue 54	**Young David** runs away in tears *Cross-fade to* **Mrs Steerforth** *and* **Rosa**	(Page 75)
Cue 55	**Rosa**: " ... for life itself." *Cross-fade to the* **Micawbers**	(Page 76)
Cue 56	**Micawber**: " ... for that distinction!" *Cross-fade to* **David**'*s rooms*	(Page 77)

Cue 57	**David**: " ... my dear aunt's investments ——" *Cross-fade to* **Micawber**	(Page 78)
Cue 58	**Micawber**: " ... into my private ear ..." *Cross-fade to* **David** and **Agnes**	(Page 79)
Cue 59	**Agnes**: "... will be stronger in the end." *Cross-fade to* **Mrs Micawber**	(Page 79)
Cue 60	**Mrs Micawber**: " ... on the twins!" *Cross-fade to a pool of light on* **Mr Peggotty**	(Page 79)
Cue 61	**Mr Peggotty**: " ... to bring her home." *Cross-fade to Highgate area*	(Page 79)
Cue 62	**Rosa**: "Show her to me." *Shaft of cold light on* **Mr Peggotty**	(Page 80)
Cue 63	**Mr Peggotty**: "Em'ly's alive!" *Bring up light on* **Emily**	(Page 80)
Cue 64	**Emily**: " ... whose wife I should have been ..." *Bring up light on* **Ham**	(Page 80)
Cue 65	The wind blows louder *Fade to black-out*	(Page 81)
Cue 66	To open SCENE 17 *Bring up general lighting on the wedding party*	(Page 81)
Cue 67	**Aunt Betsey**: "You must have patience, Trot." *Cross-fade to* **Micawber**	(Page 83)
Cue 68	**David**: " ... glass on glass of wine." *Cross-fade to* **Wickfield**'s room	(Page 84)
Cue 69	**Micawber**: " ... and doomed traitor — *Heep*!" *Cross-fade to dim light on* **Rosa** *and* **Emily**	(Page 85)
Cue 70	**Mr Peggotty** carries **Emily** away *Cross-fade to* **Dora**	(Page 87)
Cue 71	**Dora**: " ... or I shall not believe you." *Cross-fade to* **Wickfield**'s office	(Page 89)
Cue 72	**David** is left with **Dora** and **Young David** *Lighting change*	(Page 94)

| *Cue* 73 | **David**: " ... take the coach ..." | (Page 94) |
| | *Cross-fade to storm lighting* | |

| *Cue* 74 | **David**: "Steerforth ... Steerforth ..." | (Page 97) |
| | *Bring up light on* **Rosa** | |

| *Cue* 75 | **Rosa**: " ... friends to whom he stooped!" | (Page 97) |
| | *Fade light on* **Rosa***; concentrate lighting on* **David** | |

| *Cue* 76 | **Aunt Betsey**: " ... and her husband too." | (Page 97) |
| | *Bring up light on* **Agnes** | |

| *Cue* 77 | **David**: "David Copperfield ..." | (Page 98) |
| | *Fade to black-out* | |

EFFECTS PLOT

ACT I

Cue 1   The Lights come up on **David** at a desk   (Page 1)
Thunderstorm in the distance; gradually increasing

Cue 2   **David**: " ... something wanting ... always, always."   (Page 1)
Thunderstorm louder

Cue 3   **Company**: "A common vagabond ..."   (Page 1)
Thunderstorm louder

Cue 4   **David**: "... the *black void* ..."   (Page 1)
Cut thunderstorm; bring up birdsong

Cue 5   **Murdstone, Quinion** and **Passnidge** turn and go   (Page 7)
Sound of horses trotting away

Cue 6   To open SCENE 5   (Page 8)
Sound of seagulls and gentle wind

Cue 7   **Emily** runs out into the audience   (Page 10)
Sound of wind

Cue 8   **Murdstone** slams the door on **Young David**   (Page 14)
Door slam, loud sound of door being locked

Cue 9   **David**: " ... the length of those five days ..."   (Page 14)
*Sounds in sequence as **Young David** speaks: bells ringing,*
*   doors opening and shutting, voices, footsteps on stairs,*
*   laughing and singing outside*

Cue 10   **David**: "So I lost her."   (Page 15)
Sound of trotting horses; continue

Cue 11   **Barkis**: " ... Barkis is willin', would you?"   (Page 16)
Sound of horses stopping

Cue 12   **Barkis** retreats   (Page 16)
Sound of horses trotting away

Cue 13   They carry **Young David** to **Steerforth**'s door   (Page 19)
              Banging on door

Cue 14   To open SCENE 16   (Page 25)
              Sound of horses' hooves; continue

Cue 15   **David**: " ... out of my body."   (Page 26)
              Sound of horses stops

Cue 16   Loud goodbyes   (Page 27)
              Sound of horses' hooves; continue

Cue 17   **David**: " ... was stop at a church."   (Page 27)
              Sound of horses stops; birdsong, fade when ready

Cue 18   **Murdstone**: " ... and break it."   (Page 30)
              Slurp of a river, damp drip in decaying waterside building

Cue 19   **Young David**: "Oh thank you, thank you, sir!"   (Page 31)
              Cut river and dripping noise

Cue 20   **Mrs Micawber**:" ... as Papa used to say ——"   (Page 32)
              Banging from downstairs

Cue 21   **Micawber**: "Catastrophe!"   (Page 34)
              Door slam, locks locking, bolts bolting

Cue 22   **Mrs Micawber**:" ... and I never would if I could."   (Page 37)
              Sound of post-horn, departing stage coach

Cue 23   **Young David**: "NO! *No!*   (Page 38)
              Sound of shout, squeals, cart wheels, running feet, etc.

Cue 24   **Aunt Betsey**: "Donkeys!"   (Page 41)
              Loud braying

Cue 25   **Aunt Betsey**: "Donkeys!"   (Page 44)
              Loud braying

ACT II

Cue 26   To open SCENE 3   (Page 55)
              Schubert played on piano in the background

Cue 27   **Rosa**: "Well, that's quite delightful."   (Page 55)
              Cut piano music

| *Cue* 28 | The Lights fade on **Dora** | (Page 60) |
| | *Schubert played on piano in the background* | |

| *Cue* 29 | **Steerforth**: "She was born to be a lady." | (Page 60) |
| | *Cut piano music* | |

| *Cue* 30 | **Aunt Betsey** hurries off | (Page 61) |
| | *Clocks tick, distant bells ring* | |

| *Cue* 31 | **David**: "But within a week ——" | (Page 62) |
| | *Mighty hammering on the door* | |

| *Cue* 32 | **David**: " ... ladies, music ..." | (Page 64) |
| | *Party noise; continue* | |

| *Cue* 33 | **David** collapses | (Page 65) |
| | *Party noise reaches a crescendo; then fades* | |

| *Cue* 34 | **Rosa**: "Show her to me." | (Page 80) |
| | Wind starts to blow | |

| *Cue* 35 | **Mr Peggotty**: " ... afore the rest ..." | (Page 80) |
| | *Wind blows louder then fades* | |

| *Cue* 36 | The wedding veil lifts off | (Page 82) |
| | *Clock ticks* | |

| *Cue* 37 | **Micawber**: "My dear Copperfield ..." | (Page 83) |
| | *Rumble of carriage wheels, wild neighing of horses* | |

| *Cue* 38 | **David**: "' ... take the coach ... '" | (Page 94) |
| | *Distant thunderstorm, wind increasing* | |

| *Cue* 39 | **Ham**: " ... what she was." | (Page 95) |
| | *Storm increases* | |

| *Cue* 40 | **Company**: "The loud waves roaring ..." | (Page 95) |
| | *Wind, noise, waves crashing; door slam. Reduce storm noise and crashing waves; bring up sound of shutters groaning and creaking* | |

| *Cue* 41 | **David**: " ... from the black void!" | (Page 95) |
| | *Increase noise of storm, wind and waves; then reduce slightly* | |

| *Cue* 42 | **Company**: "In their boiling graves ..." | (Page 95) |
| | *Increase noise of storm, wind and waves; then reduce slightly* | |

Cue 43   **Ham**: "I'm a-going out!"   (Page 96)
            Increase noise of storm, wind and waves; then reduce
               slightly

Cue 44   **Company**: "In their boiling graves ..."   (Page 95)
            Sudden silence; when ready sudden crash of thunder and
               noise of sea; gradually fading